I

MAY

BE

WRONG

James McGuire

Published in 2017
I May Be Wrong
Copyright © James McGuire, 2017
All rights reserved

James McGuire asserts the moral right under the Copyright, Designs and Patents Act 1988 and the European Communities (Copyright and Related Rights) Regulations, 2004 to be identified as the author of this work.

ISBN 978-0-9575260-4-4

All Rights reserved. No part of this publication may be reproduced, stored in a retrieval system, or transmitted in any form or by any means without the prior written consent of the publisher, nor be otherwise circulated in any form of binding or cover than that in which it is published and without a similar condition being imposed on the subsequent purchaser. This book is a work of 'non-fiction'. This book is sold subject to the condition that it shall not, by way of trade or otherwise, be lent, resold, hired out, or otherwise circulated without the publishers prior consent in any form of binding or cover or format, other than that in which it is published and without a similar condition, including this condition, being imposed upon the subsequent purchaser.

Your support and respect for the property of this author is appreciated.

This book is a work of **non-fiction**.

"All you need is what you are and because you are, you need not"

The Beginning

This book is founded on the hypothesis that *perception is the exclusive cause of all emotional responses.* In 2010 I had a spontaneous involuntary mystical experience. I defined it as spiritual. After this experience all my fear and anxiety were gone. After this experience I was unable to respond with 'anxiety', 'fear' or 'anger' to the people and situations that normally provoked those reactions. I no longer perceived the same meaning in the same people, situations and stimulus. The contrast in how my thoughts and feelings responded to the same people and situations before and after my experience was remarkable.

It took several years for me to understand why all of my fear had gone. This book describes the therapeutic benefits obtained by consciously changing our perception of people, experiences and stimulus. The reader is encouraged to contemplate removing their faith in any belief disproven by fact. Factual or not, our beliefs have obtained our faith. *My experience was a miracle!* In my experience my mind spontaneously transformed. I came to realise the fact that the exclusive cause of every one of my 'emotional responses' was and is my own perception. This book describes how my mind was transformed.

In psychological terms I experienced cognitive change. I witnessed the transformation of my own mind. If the statements contained within this book are factually correct it implies a therapeutic methodology for the treatment of numerous psychological issues.

What I experienced was the involuntary withdrawal of the faith I had placed in all of my beliefs. This instantly dismantled numerous psychological complexes that were sustained exclusively by my faith. I once lived without peace of mind. I now control what enters and remains within my mind. Another hypothesis offered here is that *faith is the creator of all perception.*

The objective of this book is to demonstrate the power of 'faith'. A believer's faith is the doorway to their mind. It is not possible for others to place their beliefs within our mind *without our faith.* Only faith can convert a hypothesis into a personal belief. *Our power is our faith!* Each mind's expression is empowered or disempowered by the beliefs that obtain a believer's faith. There is a phrase in computer programming, 'Garbage in, garbage out!' Winner and losers are the behavioural expression of contrasting belief systems. What are beliefs? Beliefs are the existential software that controls the expression of each mind.

A belief can only be installed within the mind by obtaining a believer's faith in a hypothesis. We are all 'believers'. A belief has no power over us without our faith. Our belief system is our mind's personal operating system. The power of a belief is the faith it obtains. Faith is the most powerful thing in existence. I realised that I could remove a belief from my mind simply by withdrawing my faith in it. A belief has no control without power. The power of our beliefs is our own faith. The most evil of men are transformed by removing their faith in the beliefs that control them. Our faith allows our beliefs to control our own mind.

This book encourages the reader to recognise the

THE BEGINNING

personal constraints their own faith now places upon the expression of their own mind. What has our faith? Our beliefs have our faith! Anyone that understands how the mind works can achieve personal transformation. It is the mind that exclusively creates all symptoms defined in psychological terms. Each mind is omnipotent. We are not our mind. We are the believers spoken of in scriptures. Only our faith can authorise a belief to enter our own mind. Each mind is more valuable than anything in the world. Each and every mind is a sacred medium of direct communication with God.

Beliefs are the language of communication with God. The power of each belief is the faith it obtains. Every archetypal identity is a generic belief system. Generic belief systems were created to programme and control each mind's creative and behavioural expression. The context of this book is therapeutic. In existential terms we escape the prison of our own mind by realising that our own faith is our jailor. I realised that my faith was controlling my mind and body. I realised I was incarcerated by my mind and my mind was incarcerated by my faith. Religions are 'belief systems' originally created to protect man from man.

The realisation of my whole mind resulted from a spiritual experience. This was an experience with God. In that experience I felt the love of God. What immediately followed my experience was a sustained period of what conformed to the dictionary definition of the word 'psychosis'. The only way we can remain connected with what is generically perceived to be reality is to sustain our faith in all of the words and hypotheses that were created to define it. One day all beliefs were removed from my mind and my mind was free. Our faith in words creates a vocabulary that replaces individual experience with educated perception.

This book contains a brief explanation of my life accompanied by fifty essays on various topics. This book was not produced to teach. One of the aims of this book is to encourage the reader to question their own belief system. Each believer's mind is unlimited. *"The only thing that can constrain the expression of our unlimited mind is our own 'faith".* Unless we are disabled our mind's expression can only be limited by the beliefs that have our faith. We are all believers! Our faith is the divine architect of our own life. Our behavioural expression reveals what has our faith. This book is not about learning.   This book is about *unlearning*.

I was born in Birmingham's Selly Oak Hospital in England in 1962. My parents were Irish Catholics from the same town in Ireland. They moved to England in the late 1950s. My first memories were when I was around two years of age playing in the backyard of a building where we rented a flat. In my early years I was a happy and active child without a care in the world. I had a lot of energy. At that age my accent was Irish. At the age of three we moved to an area that did not have a large Irish community. I learned to speak with an English accent in the street whilst speaking with an Irish accent in the home.

Nearly all children have to be one way with their peers and another way in the home. This is not limited to people from different cultures or countries. I was quite outgoing until I was around six years of age. For as long as I can

The Beginning

remember I was constantly told that I should be grateful. I was told not to speak until I was spoken to and if I did something wrong I would be smacked. It was my Mother who always smacked me. In the 1960s many but not all people were of the opinion that corporal punishment was the duty of a parent. In the 1970's the cane was the main method of corporal punishment in many British schools.

Until I was around four I would forget that I had been smacked within a few minutes and so it wouldn't be long before I got smacked again. Getting smacked wasn't that painful and it was brief so I recovered within minutes to continue climbing fences and running around the streets. If I got too loud I would have to go to the back yard and stay there. I spent many hours alone in the backyard. Every one of my behaviours seemed to result in my mother's anger or criticism. My mother was unable to converse with me. If I showed emotion or looked for any emotional support I would be told that I should be grateful.

As a child I was a fussy eater. I wouldn't eat vegetables. I remember my mother talking to a priest after mass and telling him how much trouble I was. The priest told my mother that if she spared the rod she would spoil the child. I could cope with getting smacked but he seemed to be telling her that she wasn't being hard enough. To this day I have no idea what I was doing wrong. I was around four when smacking became beatings. I could also cope with the beatings because they never lasted long and so I knew that each one would be over soon enough. My coping mechanism was to repeat 'One, two, three, four,' over and over until she stopped.

Initially because of my nature and my apparent

amnesia the beatings in themselves never worked at controlling my behaviour. I was just a ball of fun. My mother was concerned about my behaviour which in her opinion was bad. She continually told me that when I grew up I wouldn't be able to get a job and would end up in prison and then go to hell. Nothing got through to me until one day the methods changed. I love my mother and I realise that she was quite limited in her world view. I do not want to give the impression of a monster. This is included here because it explains how I started to consciously control my own behaviour.

One day I did something wrong and I was told to go to my room every day after school and not come out. I don't remember if this went on for weeks or months but I began to question myself and blame myself for what had happened to me. At first the room and loneliness was extremely difficult but eventually I accepted it. Finally I began to change and the change was profound. I went from being outgoing and physically active to being introverted and inactive. I stopped mixing with people and disliked myself. Over time the method of my punishment also changed. I don't remember the exact details but one day my mother said, 'Just you wait'.

A couple of days after hearing these words I woke to my mother dragging me from my bed on to the landing where I was beaten. These warnings became my mother's most effective method of psychological control. My mother used a phrase that told me I was getting a beating. It was a very effective statement said in particular tone and, whilst those words had no meaning to anyone else, listening I knew what was coming. I

The Beginning

didn't know if it would be a day or a week but I struggled to sleep until it was over. I became anxious. The beatings only lasted a couple of minutes. It was during this period of my life that I created my fear.

I formed beliefs that created fearful responses to situations that I wanted to avoid. It kept me safe. My fear signals controlled my behaviour and my 'complex' paid off. *The beatings stopped.* The cost of my compliance was the part of 'me' that I denied. If a child denies their own natural expression it can lead to longer term inhibitions. As time went on my complex resulted in my perceiving problems and difficulties that really didn't exist. One personal complex was to perceive problems and then find solutions for them that would keep me safe. My neurosis was to perceive difficulties that did not exist outside of my own mind.

My father and mother grew up in the same town. When I was young I only saw him at weekends. He left for work when we were in bed and came home when we were in bed. My father was a functioning alcoholic. He was old school Irish. He went to work. He went to mass. He went to the pub. He expected his dinner on the table when he got home. Other than saying hello and goodbye we rarely spoke to each other. When he came home from the pub he would sit in the front room alone. He avoided us. He was more like a lodger than a dad. I liked him and would have done anything for him but he never had any time for me.

When I was young my family went to Mass every week. Mass was the same thing every week. It was a cold experience. As a small child I believed in God because I believed God existed. God never answered what I then *believed* were prayers. One day my mother told me that I had committed an immortal sin and that I could never go to heaven. It was overwhelming. I said, 'God I hate you'. I was told that I was going to hell and nothing could save me. I told God that I hated him and I wanted to die. *I believed* what I was told. I'd had enough. I didn't know how to cope. I was a very troubled little boy.

Until I was fourteen I was socially and behaviourally introverted. At fourteen I joined a small gang that had formed in my neighbourhood and we would steal cars and burgle shops. I've always had a sense of humour. I was popular because I was a laugh. My humour may have been a coping mechanism but from the moment I was born I have always loved to laugh. One of the boys living on my street that was not in our gang told one of the owners of a shop we had burgled who we were and where we lived. This led to my arrest. When the police came to arrest me one of the other lads was sitting in the back of the car.

The police asked him to show them where a particular shop was. I tried to shut him up but he wasn't able to keep quiet. We were charged with burglary and given a court date. I was fourteen years old and the year was 1977. When I appeared in court my mother asked the magistrate to put me somewhere. She said that she couldn't cope with me. I was remanded whilst assessments were carried out and returned to court three weeks later. The magistrate gave my mother a fine of £70 and I was released with a supervision order. In the gang I had found my family. I was accepted. My mates were my mates and that was all I needed.

My school reports were very poor. I truanted from school so much that I was taken out of school by social services and had to attend an attendance centre. In the attendance centre we just played table tennis and lounged around. I had a breakdown aged around nine and after this I found it almost impossible to concentrate. So I went from having some academic capability to being incapable of understanding or remembering what the teachers were saying. Everything was just too much. Everything was just too difficult. At fifteen I was arrested in my home. The charge was 'attempted take and drive away (TDA)'.

I hadn't attempted to take and drive anything away. It was 1978 and I had been out with my mates the night before. After I left them and went home they stole a tool box from a parked car. The next evening the police arrived at my house to ask me about this car and I said I was not involved. My mother told them that I was! My mother was just angry. She had completely lost all control over me. There was no love between us *then*. I wouldn't cooperate with the police but it was apparent that they had arrived at my door because someone in the gang had given them my name. I was charged.

Whilst I sat outside the court room at Birmingham Juvenile Court my social worker approached me with a barrister. The barrister seemed to be quite a nice lady and she explained that it would be better if I pleaded guilty. I said that I wasn't going to plead guilty because I hadn't done anything wrong. The barrister and my social worker explained that if I was to plead guilty it would be a fine and it would be over that day and I could go home. They said that if I did not plead guilty the case would go to Crown Court and it could go on for months. Eventually I agreed. So when I was asked how I pleaded I said 'guilty'.

Within seconds of saying those words the barrister addressed the magistrate and requested a Care Order with immediate effect until I was eighteen years of age. This lady spent fifteen minutes debating my options. She never mentioned that her objective was to have me placed in care. Her words were simply the tools of her trade. It took decades for me to realise that the police, my mother, the social worker and the barrister had all agreed on the best course of action 'for them'. *They were all liars!* I was taken from the court and held in an assessment centre for three months. I was then sent to a community home school.

In 1979 my sister's friend got me a job on a tarmac gang and I was released. I packed the job in after a few weeks and went on the dole. Whilst I wasn't guilty of the crime that got me put in care it was only a matter of time before I did commit a crime. My year inside allowed me to live without a care in the world. In my mind all that could go wrong had gone wrong. I realised the value of my freedom. I never wanted to be in that position again. After my release I started to meet up with my old mates who were still involved in petty crime. Most Friday nights would end in drunken fights and as time went on they got more violent.

I knew that if I did not get out of Birmingham I would end up in prison. In 1984 I moved to North East Derbyshire. I could relate well to people but I could not be close to

THE BEGINNING

anyone. I didn't trust anyone. In my twenties and thirties I would describe my psychological state as mildly pessimistic and my world view to be somewhat sceptical. I couldn't bond with people at an emotional level. I was not capable of feeling or expressing love. Women always wanted more than I could give. I existed. I ate, drank and slept. There was no badness in me but there was also no love in me.

Even with my lack of schooling I did eventually graduate from university. What I learned during my time at university was how to write a coursework that would get me a pass. As the years passed I acquired a number of post graduate degrees. I earned my living in the construction industry as a consultant and have worked in various locations around the world. In spite of my poor schooling I did manage to turn things around. Even with my experience I have not changed my opinions about people. The world is controlled by fear, greed and selfishness. Apart from my father I have never met an entirely honest man in my entire life.

I now live with compassion. The world could not be the way it is without a universal lack of compassion. For most of my adult life I have walked a straight line. In 2010 whilst working abroad I realised that I was not happy but I also simultaneously realised that I was not unhappy. I accepted my life as I understood it and also accepted at that time that things would never change. I realised that money, success and relationships could not make me happy. I didn't appreciate realising this because I had spent most of my life pursuing those things in the hope that they would make me happy.

In August 2010 something happened. I'd hired a van

from Heathrow Airport in the UK to move some personal possessions from England to a house I had built in Ireland. Over time the relationship with my mother had healed. My mother had given me an acre of my father's land in Ireland and I had built a house there. So I loaded the van and drove over to my house in Ireland. Immediately upon my arrival in Ireland I had to fly to London for a short trip. So I parked the van at Knock Airport in County Mayo and flew to London, planning to return a week later to collect the van and drive it back to Heathrow Airport.

This meant taking the van back to England on the ferry. So on the morning of 20th August 2010 I flew from London back to Knock Airport. The flight took about an hour. From Knock I drove the van up to my house in County Donegal which took about ninety minutes. I spent approximately an hour packing a bag and then started on the three and half hour drive across country to the Dublin Ferry Terminal. On the ferry crossing I couldn't sleep so I read a book from cover to cover. We arrived at Holyhead in the UK just after midnight. It was 21 August 2010. This is how I remember these events which may factually differ slightly.

By the time I arrived at Holyhead I had been travelling for about eight hours. I switched the van's radio on to keep myself awake. About an hour into the drive I started to feel strange. Sad music seemed to make me feel sad. I then started to feel upset so I turned the radio off but I was so tired that I had to turn it back on again. At around 3 a.m. whilst driving south on the M6 motorway I started to feel odd. I questioned what I was feeling and remembered that I had felt this feeling once before when I was ill. I had the thought that I was dying

THE BEGINNING

and within seconds I heard a voice in my head.

The voice said that I did not have much time left and that I was experiencing my final moments. I got upset but continued driving at a speed of around seventy miles an hour. The vehicle was weaving in and out of the white lines that separated the carriageway lanes and I was losing and gaining speed. I don't know how I did not crash the vehicle. I struggled to remain conscious and awake whilst driving. At one point I was looking down at my body as I was being pulled out of it feet first. I tightened my grip on the steering wheel and held on for my life whilst simultaneously being in my body looking out at the road ahead.

I said out loud that I wanted to say goodbye. I was then told by this voice that I did not have much time and that I should do this 'now'. I then took out my phone whilst still driving. I was now becoming distraught. I broke down in tears and began to look for a number to call friends to tell them that I loved them, but I couldn't do it. This was the first time I realised that I loved anyone. I then got prompted again by this voice which said that I didn't have much time. I said I can't make the call, because if I call people when they hear that I have died they may think that I committed suicide and that my call was a cry for help.

I was looking for a motorway services sign so that I could pull off the road. The voice then asked '*What would you say to those you love if you could speak to them now*'? The first words that came out of my mouth were my own. I said "I would tell them that I love them" followed by the involuntary statement "and I feel the Love of God in me" which were not my chosen words.

I then had what I can only describe as a heart attack. It was not a heart attack of pain. It was a feeling of pure love. I felt love enter and fill my heart like water would fill a glass and that feeling of love was beyond anything I had experienced in my entire life.

In that moment I felt love for the first time. In that moment I knew it was the Love of God. I believed in God before this moment but *I do not believe in God now!* I do not believe in God because I now know that God is real. *You can only believe what you do not know.* After a few minutes this feeling of love faded but it has never fully left me. I realised that I was not going to die that night. Something died in the van that night but it was not me. What died was my fear. In physical and emotional terms I felt extremely vulnerable after this experience. I didn't know how but I knew that things would never be the same again.

I have already written my testimony which was written during a period of what is most accurately described using the term 'psychosis'. My testimony reveals what was being shown to me in my dreams in the weeks and months following my experience. This book is not based upon the realisations of someone in the throes of a spiritual awakening. *I am awake!* My experience revealed a 'therapeutic process'. This book explains the awakening and realisation process that I experienced. This book has not been written to teach. This book is written to remind people so that they can remember their own innate power and wisdom.

When I returned the van to Heathrow Airport I retreated to my house in Ireland and shut the door. I felt wonderful but extremely vulnerable. For the first two months my eyes would see what I had seen before but I could not consciously remember the words for anything that I looked at. I felt wonderful and at peace. I avoided being around people. The happiness I felt was a feeling that I had not experienced in my entire life. I experienced a profound transformation in the months and years that followed. In the initial weeks following my experience my dreams were disturbing. After a period of time I began to write them down. One of the first things I remember writing was

"You can only believe what you do not know because when you know you have no need of beliefs because you know."

In the weeks following my experience I could not consciously remember the names of everyday things. I contemplated that I may be suffering from dementia. After two months I flew to Peru and drank Ayahuasca. Ayahuasca showed me what I was going to go through but it did not do the work for me. I returned from Peru and again I shut my door and my dreams continued to reveal all sorts of things. I was being educated and I was a willing student. Before my experience my perception of people who I liked would generate pleasant feelings and my perception of people who I did not like would generate unpleasant feelings.

After my experience I could not feel bad. Even when I thought about those who had stolen from me or lied to me or dumped me I understood why and I felt nothing but compassion. I eventually realised that my feelings had never responded to those people or those situations. My feelings had responded to my perception of those people and situations. I realised that in my entire life I had never been unhappy. So my question to God was well if I have never been unhappy why did I feel unhappy? My interpretation of the answer is that my feelings were the neurochemical effect of my judgement of those people and those situations.

In simple terms if I judged something to be good I felt good and if I judged something to be bad I felt bad. If I judged something to be boring I felt bored. If I judged something to be disgusting, I felt disgusted. My feelings were reflecting my judgement of the world. My feelings were neurochemical responses controlled by my judgement. I called each neurochemical response a feeling and defined each feeling to be an emotion. I could be frustrated, angry, disgusted, unhappy and fearful. My perception caused every feeling that was not peace, joy or happiness. I was also shown where this was revealed in the scriptures.

MATTHEW 7:1-2 KJV *"Judge that you be not judged. For with what judgment ye judge, ye shall be judged: and with what measure ye mete, it shall be measured to you again."* I asked God if the Bible was the word of God and in my mind I was told that it was *'not the word of God'* but *'it contains the word of God'*. Man is incarcerated by his vocabulary which establishes the limits of his understanding. God's expression is not limited by man's vocabulary. I was shown evil acts such as murder, rape, dismembering, stoning, crucifixion, slavery, cruelty, paedophilia, manipulation and theft. A 'merciful God' does not commit *evil acts*.

I was shown that the God of the scriptures is merciful and compassionate. I realised that my 'compassion' would show me which words in the scriptures revealed a scribe of God and which revealed the devil's hand. It is by obtaining a believer's faith in violent beliefs that you create a violent mind. MATTHEW 7:15 KJV *"Beware of false prophets, which come to you in sheep's clothing, but inwardly they are ravening wolves."* There were stages to my awakening. Some of these stages felt horrific. One day my peace and joy ended as abruptly as it began. One day all of my judgemental beliefs were returned to my mind.

All my fear returned and I thought my whole spiritual experience was just my imagination. I was back to normal. I felt that God had abandoned me. *Had I just imagined this?* To be healed and free of all judgement was wonderful but to have my mind repopulated with the old beliefs that were the cause of my unhappiness was horrific. Not only did the old emotional responses return but they appeared to be amplified and a nightmare began. I asked God what good is it to give me joy only to take it back and let me return to what I was before? Each thought or feeling reflected what I believed about this person or that situation.

I got upset and angry. I had no control over my emotional responses. I felt fear. Then I remembered that without my faith I could not be upset by any belief. I began to consciously question the cause of every feeling that felt bad. I noticed that my feelings stopped responding to people and situations when I realised that the cause of my responses was 'not true'. I began to consciously question the cause of every emotional response that felt bad. When I realised that what I believed to be the cause of my distress was not true those emotional responses ceased revealing a peaceful mind and body. *I realised!*

For my entire life my own faith was the exclusive cause of my emotional responses. I also realised that my faith gave my beliefs full control over all of my 'emotional responses'. What I believed about an experience was a prescription for a specific emotional response. To control my emotions each belief had to obtain 'my faith'. To remain within my mind each belief required my faith. Our emotional responses to people and situations cease when we withdrew our faith in the beliefs that we hold about them. In an instant I fully realised. I experienced a miracle. I was so overwhelmed that for days my only words were *'Oh my God'.*

I realised that my initial state of bliss after my spiritual experience was God showing me the cause of my unhappiness *by temporarily removing it.* If I wanted my salvation I had to do the work. The work is the removal of our faith in our beliefs. My 'perception' had caused all of my emotional responses. My perception reflected what I believed. All beliefs require faith. When all beliefs were removed from my mind I experienced the miracle of a peaceful mind and body. God will not choose for us. My beliefs were returned so that I could voluntarily remove my faith in them and accept my salvation or *continue to cause my own suffering.*

The Beginning

This was not an easy process. At times I said that I would not wish this experience on anyone. Over time I began to feel more peaceful. There were also times when I wondered if this process would ever end. Some of the old unconscious beliefs that came into my awareness were very difficult to feel. The mind of each believer is possessed by his beliefs. The removal of my faith revealed the greater understanding that each belief concealed. At one time rather than go on I contemplated taking my own life. My feelings were God's response to my judgement. Our beliefs are prescriptions for feelings that our faith assures.

I felt things that were very difficult to feel. I was exorcising my beliefs. Early in the process I realised that each day following a difficult exorcism I would feel wonderful. Exorcising a belief from my mind could feel extremely difficult but those feelings did not last. Each believer's mind without exception is controlled by their beliefs. It is not God but our own faith that condemns us. Our ability to read and write is determined by our knowledge of the words of a dictionary. The expression of the world's greatest debaters is limited only by their vocabulary. Education seeks to ensure that we all believe that each word is fact.

We are educated to believe that each word in the dictionary is what it represents. Each word is created to ensure that our minds only perceive the 'official definition'. Words attempt to define something that is beyond definition by dividing it. The dictionary is an existential software programme for the mind that replaces natural awareness with cognition. Cognition controls perception.

All emotions that are not peace, joy or happiness are *perceptually induced neurochemical responses*. I came to realise that many of the concepts that we take for granted are demonic. A demonic concept is any concept that lacks compassion.

A demonic concept is a belief that vicariously controls a believer by impelling them to deny their compassion. A demonic concept requires our faith before it can enter our mind. Our faith in concepts that lack compassion allows those concepts to enter our mind. The demonic concepts of 'enemy', 'untouchable', 'patriotism', 'terrorist', 'infidel', 'consumer', 'debtor', 'creditor' and 'pornography' allow spiritual parasites to use our faith to vicariously kill, maim, rape, enslave and exploit. We cannot have lasting peace in the world as long as just one of us places our faith in beliefs that result in the expression of these concepts.

As the years have passed my mind has gradually transformed. When we withdraw our faith in our beliefs we remove their control over our mind and body. When I no longer believed what I believed I realised myself whole as I was created. When I no longer had a single belief to define myself I realised that every single belief that had my faith was a limitation. Our faith is the only doorway through which beliefs can enter our mind. In mortal life what we believe about our self we become. Our faith allows beliefs to control our thoughts and behaviour. Our mind is sanctified when the greater understanding of God replaces our beliefs.

God is love. Fear cannot be where love is. Love cannot be where fear is but love can take the place of fear. *No man of God can feel fear*. There are many who say they believe in God but have fear. A belief *cannot enter* our mind without our faith. A belief *cannot remain* within our mind without our faith. A belief in God means that we do not know God. Religious men who do not follow the rules of their religion are hypocrites who are unbelievers. A compassionate man that has no faith in God is closer to God than any man who kills. Our mind is the altar of God where our prayers are always heard and always answered.

Every belief that has our faith is a prayer. It is not possible for a man who believes in God's commandments to break them. When we know God we no longer believe in God. Knowing and believing are not the same. *We can only believe what we do not know.* A mother does not believe her child is her child because she knows. Faith makes real what we do not know. Faith makes real what does not yet exist. What has our faith has our power. What is faith? Faith is the power of God. The metaphorical symbols of faith are magic wands, philosopher's stones and alchemy. Faith is spiritual alchemy. God has always rewarded our faith.

If our mind was not incarcerated by language we would not need to look to books for our wisdom and guidance. Our Father in heaven has never denied us. Each belief about our self that has our faith is a 'prayer' that God has always answered. *I'm not good enough* is a prayer answered. *I'm never going to be able to do that* is a prayer answered. *They are my enemy* is a prayer answered. We have been tricked and manipulated by those who understand the power of our mind. We were tricked into believing we were limited. God created our limitations in response to our prayers. Our beliefs are our prayers and our mind is God's altar.

Most minds are occupied by a generic belief system. Our own faith has condemned us to a life prescribed by our beliefs. Salvation results from the renewing of our mind. ROMANS 12:2 KJV *"And be not conformed to this world: but be ye transformed by the renewing of your mind, that ye may prove what is that good, and acceptable, and perfect, will of God."* When there is nothing in our mind but God then everything we do is an expression of the will of God. I am happy! What is happiness? Happiness is the expression of the Love of God. I exorcised the beliefs that 'trespassed' within my mind by removing my faith in them.

Our own psychological fear and anxiety is something that only we can create. I created my fear in response to events in my life. My fear enabled me to avoid the thing feared. The fact is that it is our own faith that creates and sustains our psychological complexes. We create the emotions that mask our peace, joy and happiness. What this means is that we are responsible for what we feel. Our faith is the only power that can destroy our own peace of mind. We do this by placing our faith in beliefs that lack compassion. Each belief is a prayer to God. God answers all our prayers. We are living proof of the power of our faith.

Our faith in God is not required for God's existence. To understand the power of our faith is to understand the power of God. HEBREWS 11.1 KJV *"Now faith is the substance of things hoped for, the evidence of things not seen."* To believe that *we cannot* guarantees this result. Any unopposed belief placed on the altar of our mind is

THE BEGINNING

a prayer that will be answered. To believe we are not good enough, popular enough, good looking enough or successful enough results in those outcomes. To then blame God for answering those prayers or say that God does not exist is *insane*. Authorities control us by installing their hypotheses into our minds.

Authorities are 'unbelievers' whose *official secrets* require them to conceal facts by means of deception. Our life is God's response to what has our faith. So what is faith? LUKE 13:19 *"It is like a grain of mustard seed, which a man took, and cast into his garden; and it grew, and waxed a great tree; and the fowls of the air lodged in the branches of it."* The garden of our mind is fertile soil. Each belief is a seed. Only our faith can germinate what is placed within our mind. Good or bad we are responsible for our life. MATTHEW 7:17 KJV *"Even so every good tree bringeth forth good fruit; but a corrupt tree bringeth forth evil fruit."*

Our life is our own responsibility. The walls of a prison are no match for the power of faith because faith is the power of God. Even those now incarcerated within government prisons around the world can realise salvation. Money, sex, drugs, food and rest are nothing compared to the joy that is realised when we remove our faith in all beliefs that deny our own compassion. Forgiveness is the withdrawal of faith in our beliefs. Forgiveness is how we save our self from our self. We are our own saviour. The second coming refers to each one of us. For centuries authorities used our faith to replace us with an archetypal identity.

Our minds are possessed and controlled by conflicting beliefs. The way to rediscover our own peace, joy and happiness is simple but not easy. So how do we start? To transcend all psychological complexes we must first pay attention to what we feel. We must always question *what feels bad.* If what we feel is not peace, joy or happiness then as the creator of those feelings we should always question their cause. Our own story and justification reveals the *alleged* cause. The justification for our fear, anger, anxiety, hatred, jealousy, despondency and helplessness is not fact but because *it has our faith.*

Even if we are robbed, raped or attacked by an individual, members of a group, race, colour or religion *we should not blame them all.* Religious bigotry and racism is caused by replacing everyone with a single 'archetype'. Archetypes prevent the mind seeing what is unique about any individual who conforms to an archetype. The hatred we feel for others is always a neurochemical attack on our self. Archetypes cannot exist outside of a mind. We exorcise an archetype from our mind and our world by withdrawing our faith in it. Whenever we feel bad we must always ask our self why? Then we must ask *'Is this fact'?*

When we admit that a belief is not fact its power is extinguished because its power is our faith. Placing our faith in the limiting beliefs of others allows them to use our brain's neurochemistry to control us by controlling what we feel. Peace of mind is restored when the beliefs that cause bad feelings are removed from our mind. Each neurochemical response is a feeling that in most cases will 'feel bad'. Placing our faith in positive or good beliefs will not exorcise demonic beliefs. It is by withdrawing all faith in beliefs that lack compassion that peace is restored to our mind and body. Our own faith is *our victimiser.*

This means that our faith makes us *our own victim.* Our thoughts and behaviour cannot exceed the limits placed upon our expression by the beliefs that have our faith. Our beliefs control the expression of our mind for the period of time that those beliefs have our faith. *I can't* becomes *I can* simply by removing our faith in *I can't.* Many place their faith in *I can* but do not remove their faith *I cannot* creating what are commonly defined as complexes presented by a patient to a therapist as a difficulty or problem. Our life is the effect of what has our faith. Those who rule the world do not want us to realise two things.

The first is that only our own faith has the power to control our mind. The second thing is that there are no limits to the power of our faith. Each believer's life is a testimony to the beliefs that have their faith. Our life is a reflection of what has our faith. Each believer without exception is the 'divine architect' of their own life. Religion, education and politics compete to obtain our faith in beliefs that were created to control our mind. It is by obtaining a believer's faith in a belief system that you vicariously control the expression of their mind. The educational objective is to programme each child's creative and behavioural expression.

Our life is our mind's greatest masterpiece. Our mind is controlled by our beliefs. Our beliefs can only control us for as long as they have our faith. We have allowed others to tell us what to believe. Our faith has allowed others to become the authors of the story of our life. The limits placed upon our mind's expression are sustained exclusively by the beliefs that obtain our faith. To believe that we can means that we can. To believe we cannot means that we cannot. To realise we can is to know that we can. When we know that we know, we know. Those with compassion cannot use the power of their faith to intentionally harm others.

The Ten Commandments were created to be observed by those who had not yet surrendered to their compassion. The power of faith means that we cannot fail to convert our beliefs into our experience. Faith without wisdom is faith without compassion. Wealth is an effect. Success is an effect. Poverty is an effect. Unhappiness is an effect. Sickness is an effect. So what are the causes of these effects? The cause of all of these outcomes is our own faith. What ensures a specific outcome is a specific belief. A belief is only a belief when it has faith. What is faith? Faith is the power of God given to man. Faith is the power of God in man.

A belief without faith has no power. A belief without desire is impotent. A belief without faith is a hypothesis. A belief that has our faith has our power. Those with power over us know that without our faith they are powerless. The losing candidate simply lacked faith. The electorate's faith in the winning candidate is always the cause of the election win. Faith is the creator of success, fame, poverty, wealth, loneliness, unhappiness and depression. What these terms describe are archetypal models of existence. We have never failed at converting what we

The Beginning

believe about our self into our life experience.

Our faith is sustaining limited archetypal models of existence. It is not possible for a believer's mind to contemplate possibilities that exceed what they believe to be possible. Establishing controls that limit our mind's expression is essential to any religion or government if they are to control us. You control a believer by obtaining his faith in various hypotheses. For centuries religions have used faith in religious beliefs to control the expression of those within their jurisdiction. Mind control is only possible by controlling cognition. The main tools used to control a believer's mind are language and beliefs.

Why is our faith so important to others? Faith controls the mind! We trust those we believe. We do not trust those we do not believe. Why is trust important to us? At an unconscious level we know that what has our faith has our power. Trust is to give our power over to others. For thousands of years we have been told what to believe. Our faith has allowed others to programme our minds. Many have fought and died in wars *for the beliefs of others*. All beliefs have equal power. The power of a belief is its faith. A phobia demonstrates the power of faith. The power that sustains a phobia is equal to the faith of any other belief.

Our faith can empower anything. Our faith can give all of our power to something that without our faith has no power. We can believe that a button on our coat, or a dog, a mouse or an ant can destroy us. Our beliefs are as powerful as an army of ten thousand because the power of our beliefs is our own faith. We are manipulated by those who define archetypes to be happy, successful, intelligent, creative, confident, unstoppable, kind, beautiful and sexy. We are encouraged to emulate or aspire to the archetypes promoted by the media, government and education. Why? We are enough! We are everything!

Until we realise that we can do anything we are more likely to express generic archetypal behaviours. The majority of people express the behaviours of what they would define to be an unsuccessful archetype. Our self-perception can lead to self-condemnation. Our feelings reflect what we perceive in our self and our experiences. What we perceive is always reflecting what we believe. We can only objectively see facts. Sight and perception are not the same. One is seen and the other is projected. With the exception of grief and compassion our perception is the exclusive cause of all emotional responses that mask our happiness.

A complex is a belief system. All belief systems are therefore complexes. Our opinion reflects our unique personal complex. For example, if a person who wishes to become wealthy believes that they need to get a degree then their faith in that belief creates the conditions that must be met before their mind will express the behaviour that creates wealth. Our perception is our version. Our perception always reflects what we believe. Our faith prevents our mind from achieving what we believe to be *impossible*. To believe I cannot succeed means I can't. Our mind's expression cannot exceed the jurisdiction of our own faith.

If I believe I can, *I can*. I can tie my own shoe laces. I can put on my own clothes. The fact that I do this every day means that I also have discipline. The fact that we

THE BEGINNING

all do this means that we do not lack discipline. After an initial period of disciplining our self with behavioural repetition that behaviour will require no conscious effort. In many contexts we have been educated to believe that there are certain things we cannot or should not do. The fact is most children learn to speak without any formal education. This is evidence of an inherent creative and behavioural potential that requires no conscious effort or formal education.

It is by realising *what we are* that we experience personal transformation. To realise transformation requires us to understand how spiritual alchemy works. Our faith can create anything in our mind. It was the faith of Einstein, Ford, Tesla and the Wright brothers that painted their creations in their own minds as 'ideas' before they were expressed in the world. Our faith is how we convert all of our ideas into experience. This is a fact! Many of the patents created in Tesla's mind have not yet been expressed in the world. The Wright Brothers' aircraft was first created in the mind. All technologies are first created in the mind.

The blueprint is not the origin of the idea. Faith is the origin of the idea. Henry Ford is credited with saying, *"Whether you think you can or your think you can't, you're right"*. This statement is a hypothesis that explains what 'faith' is. Faith is what powers the mind. To acquire knowledge from formal education means that our understanding is academic. Knowledge may or may not be what we know. Knowledge that comes from books that is not tested through experience is what we believe, *not what we know*. Every belief system establishes the personal limits of each mind's voluntary expression.

Every belief system is a 'complex'. If we believe we can do anything and have a strong desire then nothing and nobody can stop us. Faith and behaviour is how we convert what we believe into what we achieve. Education, religions, institutions and legislation were created to place dogmatic constraints within our minds. The reasons for using generic beliefs to enforce generic behavioural expression are justified by reliance on 'moral concepts'. Faith in dogma ensures that we do not realise the power of our whole mind. If we all wake up then no government, religion, ideology, group or army can prevent the transformation of the world.

We are all Christ. We are all Buddha. We are all criminals. We are all evil. We are all good. We are each and all everything. What we express will depend on what we believe about our self and the World. This is why religions, governments and the media compete to obtain our faith. Our beliefs are our 'prayers' and our prayers are always answered. Our mind is the altar where our faith offers up our prayers. God answers each and every prayer. If we believe we cannot, so be it. If we believe we need to get a degree to get a job, so be it. If we believe the world is evil, so be it. If we believe we are ugly, so be it.

The power of the faith of each of us is equal. To use our power without compassion means that we lack wisdom. We can only want to change until we realise what we are. God has never denied us. It was always our own faith that denied us. Prayers require faith. Our beliefs have our faith. Our beliefs are prayers and our prayers are always answered. The power of faith is unlimited. Faith without desire is to place our faith in someone else's beliefs or desires. With power comes responsibility. If what has our faith has our power and what we believe has our faith, then if we believe we can seduce our neighbour's wife, *we can*.

This is why the Ten Commandments were created. This is why we must not break God's commandments which were all *created out of compassion*. This is why we must not covet our neighbour's house, wife or possessions. If we use our power without compassion we may cheat, lie, steal, rob, attack, rape or murder. If we place information in the minds of others that we know is neither truth nor fact then we use their faith to lead them astray. This is why we should not bear false witness. A thief has not realised his own power. Every single product was first created in the mind as an idea. Our beliefs control our mind because they have our faith.

Faith is omnipotent. The source of every blueprint in the world is an idea. The source of all ideas is God. Ideas are God's response to what has our faith. The value of a mind is not determined by academic results. The creative potential of a man is not established by reference to his academic credentials. The value of a man is what has his faith. The faith of each mind is 'equal'. The power of each mind is equal. If the power of each mind is equal why do some of us live in slums whilst others live in mansions? The contrasting fortunes of poverty and wealth are caused by the *specific beliefs* that obtain a believer's faith.

Our beliefs are the ingredients of a belief system. The recipes for poverty and wealth require different ingredients. Those ingredients are beliefs that must obtain our faith. It is the ingredients of our mind that determines its expression. The house we live in, the food we eat, the car we drive and the quality our relationships are the effects of the beliefs that have our faith. To transform our life we must transform our mind. We are born innocent so that we may acquire wisdom through experience. Innocence is an empty mind. We are victims of nothing more than our own faith. That means we are not victims. *We are creators!*

If we are not happy it is because we are *mis-creating*. The 'placebo' effect is the power of faith. If we believe we can be healed by the pill we will be healed by the pill. If we do not believe we can be healed by the pill we cannot be healed by the pill. Fear is the power of faith. A phobia is the power of faith. Hate is the power of faith. All psychological maladies are sustained by the faith we have placed in what we believe about our self and the world. We experience transformation by removing our faith in our beliefs.

The second part of this book is fifty essays. The essays reveal some of my observations from my perspective *now*. They can be read sequentially or as stand alone essays.

A Life Unfulfilled	1
Addiction	6
Alpha and Omega	11
An Incarcerated Mind	15
Archetypes and the Mind	19
Comfort Zone and Addiction	25
Conditioned Responses	28
Conviction	33
Crime and Poverty	36
Demons	41
Do Unto Others	45
Duality and Non-Duality	50
Experience is God's Response to Faith	56
Faith Creates Poverty or Wealth	65
Faith is God's Power	70
Foundations of Clay	73
Heaven	77
Hell	88
I can or I cannot is a Choice	91
Idolatry	95
Love is not an Emotion	98
Love	101
Power	104
Real and Illusion	109
Realisation	112

Rejecting the World	115
Religion and Psychosis	121
Salvation or Damnation	129
Success	135
The Devil	140
The Dream of Life	151
The Dream	161
The Effect of Criticism	165
The Existential Prison	170
The Faith of a Grain of Mustard Seed	173
The Fallacy of Archetypes	177
The Flower	186
The Good and the Bad	189
The Kingdom of Heaven	193
The Pull of Addiction	197
The Sacred Paradox	203
Thought	206
To be Born Again	209
Tolerance	213
We Create Our Life	216
What Causes Conflict	220
What is Evil?	225
What is Forgiveness?	228
Why Duality?	231
Zero	246

A Life Unfulfilled

An awake mind is one that has disconnected from all beliefs and words that define reality for long enough to undo all 'psycho-emotional' relationships. Once the mind defines what it is experiencing it defines the cause of the experience. This creates a relationship that determines how our mind responds to what it defines. Love, peace and joy are not emotions but what we naturally feel. A new born child will demonstrate that unless there is hunger or physical discomfort then love, peace and joy is our natural state. Pain is not an emotion.

Pain is how the mind and body communicates. Pain is a feeling that is not emotional. A mind awake is no longer a victim of mind-made emotional responses. Ask just one person whose life has spanned some seventy years how many days did they experience physical pain and physical infirmity? For each person the answer will be different. Most will have forgotten about any 'real' pain they experienced in physical terms. Ask the same person how many days in their life have they felt unhappy, fearful, anxious, depressed, sad, regretful or wished for a different life.

For most people the answer is that they have felt pain for no more than a few weeks over the period of their entire life but this number will be multiplied many times to calculate the amount of days that they claim their life felt unhappy, difficult, depressing, unfulfilled and was a 'struggle'. This is simply *not fact*. It was fear alone that stole those years of peace. People who claim to have spent their life feeling unhappy simply haven't realised. They haven't realised it is impossible to feel the generic emotions defined as 'unhappiness' unless our mind judges its experience.

If we have an expectation of people then we have created the criterion and cause of the feeling we have defined as 'disappointment'. It is not possible to feel what we have defined using the word disappointment without an implied or explicit expectation. Expectation alone is the exclusive cause of the stimulus response that is felt and defined using the word 'disappointment'. If we expect to celebrate a win, pass an exam, find love, get a job, we define the 'acceptable'. We also imply and qualify the unacceptable that triggers pre-programmed emotional responses.

If we get what we expect and desire, our peace of mind is sustained and we do not attack ourselves in emotional terms with our own body's chemistry but reward the body with 'good' feelings. All emotions are *perceptually induced chemical responses* that are pre-programmed by our beliefs. When we or others do not live up to our expectations in religious, social, societal, academic, romantic, financial, lifestyle or parental' terms, those expectations will trigger responses in our brain that we feel in our body and define using emotional terms.

If we encountered a previously undiscovered primitive community in the Amazon Rainforest how many of them would be capable of feeling disappointment, despondency, depression, anxiety or a sense of unfulfilled potential? We cannot judge people or experience without explicit or implied expectations for behavioural or experiential compliance. Expectation places conditions upon our peace, joy and happiness. It is the beliefs held within the mind about any stimulus that exclusively determine which chemicals the brain releases as a stimulus response that is *felt*.

The feeling of disappointment is a pre-programmed stimulus response. All mind made emotions are pre-programmed stimulus responses. Love, grief, peace, joy and happiness are NOT mind made emotions. Disappointment is just one of many mind made feelings commonly defined by the generic word 'emotion'. Emotions are not feelings that are natural but feelings that were created by the mind's own judgement of its perceived self and what it perceives that self to be experiencing. We pray to God so that we can realise that we are the answer to our prayers.

God is a reflection of the inner wisdom that we deny when we judge *what is* to be less than *what it should be*. So if *it* is judged 'good' we feel good and if *it* is judged bad, boring, disgusting, unacceptable or sad we create those stimulus responses. We must forgive the stimulus our beliefs have defined using those terms so that peace can be restored to our mind and body. We have been educated to experience the world in terms that limit us. These terms are placed within our mind by others and they trespass there as judgement that controls the perception that controls our feelings.

When we withdraw our faith in any belief it loses its power over us and our mind. To remove our faith in beliefs about those who have hurt us may be difficult until we realise that we must 'forgive'. Until we forgive, our mind will use the concept of 'justification' to continue to create the stimulus responses defined as feelings of fear, unhappiness, anxiety, hatred, dislike and enmity. This is why we forgive those who trespass against us. Forgiveness frees our mind from a spiritual contract. The contract requires our faith in a belief. In return for our faith the belief creates specific feelings.

The belief is the criterion that the mind must react to when perception detects that we have been exposed to what that belief has judged. We effectively create a stimulus response that triggers thoughts and feelings for as long as we blame and condemn others. *Judge that you be not judged*. Each time we think about a person, place or thing our beliefs hold to be guilty it is an instruction to our brain to attack our body with its own feelings. God, not sharing the believer's perspective, sees beyond the prejudices that trespass within the mind. We are incarcerated by our own judgement.

We cannot become what we are. To realise 'I' we must 'be it'. A life unfulfilled is a life of delusion. What we strive to become is something that we believe 'we are not'. We have not realised that we are, always were and always will be what we wish to become. Within the whole mind separation from anything in creation is impossible. Separation was created by believing that what was within the mind existed outside of it. We are what 'who' claims to represent. The identity is the 'who' and its beliefs are trespassing within our mind.

'Who' is an identity that impersonates and incarcerates the true self for as long as we believe *it* is what we are. We remain a victim within our own mind for

A Life Unfulfilled

as long as our mind believes what it believes. We are the 'believer' written about in religious books. Each believer's mind is programmed and controlled by its beliefs. To awaken from our victimhood we must realise that whilst a belief requires a believer for its existence, a believer requires no beliefs for his existence. Without our faith in the beliefs that trespass within our mind they cease to exist and peace is restored.

Addiction

The cause of addiction is faith. Our faith creates, sustains and changes our body's *neurochemical responses*. All emotional responses are neurochemical responses. Happiness is a *pre-belief* neurochemical state also known as 'innocence'. If we were to draw a straight line a metre long and place 'happiness' at one end and 'suicidal despondency' at the other it would illustrate the archetypal extremes of human emotion. People generally exist somewhere between happiness and despondency. In simple terms when we perceive what we define to be good, we feel good, and when we perceive what we define to be bad, we feel bad.

The terms we use to describe how we feel are many and varied. Over a lifetime people can experience feelings such as depression, fear, grief, happiness, joy, excitement, sadness and anger. Our feelings define the quality of our *spiritual life*. People are generally not aware of the fact that when we place our faith in fixed beliefs we are programming our brain to respond with fixed neurochemical responses. In biological terms our emotional responses to people and stimulus are 'perceptually induced neurochemical responses'. All emotional responses are reactions to how we perceive our self, other people, situations and experiences.

You control a child's emotional responses by controlling their mind. Education is used to control a child's mind by programming it. When our perception is fixed our emotional responses become *fixed*. For example, if we perceive an activity to be boring we feel bored. If we perceive an activity to be difficult it feels difficult for us to engage in or enjoy that activity. Our feelings reflect our spiritual health. An addict uses addictive stimulus in an attempt to restore their natural state of mind. Our perception prevents our *spiritual freedom*. An 'addictive stimulus' allows an addict to access feelings denied by their own perception.

Addictive stimuli can be anything that creates 'better' feelings. Our recognition of the effect of a particular addictive stimulus on our feelings is unconscious but immediate. An addict is a *spiritual aspirant*. An addict has not realised that their perception is the cause of their 'bad feelings'. Perception is a prescription for a neurochemical response that each brain instantly dispenses. Our emotions reveal our perception. Emotions are neurochemical responses that reveal the quality of our *spiritual life*. Pain is not an emotion. A belief cannot enter our mind to programme our emotional responses unless we give that belief our faith.

In psychological terms, unhappiness is a *perceptually induced emotional response*. In biological terms unhappiness is a *perceptually induced neurochemical response*. Only our own judgement can deny us our own happiness. It is our judgement that denies us our divine inheritance. Peace, joy and happiness are our divine inheritance. The only 'facts' that feelings of anxiety, anger, resentment or unhappiness reveal is our own judgement. Every single life is an expression of this divine law. Our feelings always reveal what has our faith. Our faith is the only thing powerful enough to deny us our own happiness.

Happiness is an absence of all of the antonyms that

sustain a vocabulary that trespasses within our own mind. Emotions are simply our brain's response to our mind's perception. The explanations that rationalise or justify what we feel may be 'truthful' but not factual. To speak truthfully is to express our understanding with integrity. If what we believe about our self causes our unhappiness then we are victimised by our own faith. Our natural feelings are peace, joy and happiness. To place our faith in the belief that we possess or lack qualities will cause us to 'like' or 'dislike' our self. The cause of all man's suffering is man's faith.

A belief cannot exist within a believer's mind without a believer's faith. Our forgiveness releases us from *spiritual incarceration* sustained exclusively by our faith in our beliefs. We forgive by withdrawing our faith in all beliefs that cause us to feel bad. Our beliefs sustain our judgement. Our judgement has programmed our emotional responses. MATTHEW 7:1-3 "*Judge not, that ye be not judged. For with what judgment ye judge, ye shall be judged: and with what measure ye mete, it shall be measured to you again. And why beholdest thou the mote that is in thy brother's eye, but considerest not the beam that is in thine own eye?*"

Forgiveness is derived from the word 'shbag'. Shbag is the removal of faith in beliefs that control the mind. Each belief's control of the mind is undone by the removal of faith. Addiction is demonic. Addiction is a demon that masquerades as happiness in order to create, enslave and destroy the addict. The beliefs that have our faith will lead us to our damnation or our salvation. Addicts are incarcerated within their own mind, held there 'in hell' by their own faith. Our life experience is the direct effect of the beliefs that have our faith. We have given our faith to beliefs that we call truth. Beliefs obtain faith by masquerading as fact.

We can only believe what we do not know. Forgiveness is the removal of our faith in our beliefs. The path to our own salvation starts by *questioning what feels bad*. In the moment we experience an emotion that feels bad we should always ask our self '*Why*'? This type of questioning reveals the beliefs that have our faith. Our story is the cause and justification for why we create our unhappiness. Beliefs create perception. Perception controls our brain's neurochemical responses. Each belief is a binding spiritual contract that requires us to give our faith in return for the behavioural expression that is empowered by that belief.

The real meaning of forgiveness is *withdrawal of faith*. Beliefs require faith. A cultural or family 'feud' is sustained because of the stories that are passed down and believed. A belief is a link in a metaphorical chain that incarcerates man within his own mind. Nothing is more powerful than faith. Physical pain is real pain but every 'bad' emotional response is the effect of our own perception. Our faith is our jailor. If we do not feel happy it is because we are suffering from the effects of an illness of the mind. The cure to the illness of man's collective mind will not be found in pharmaceutical products that mask or change our neurochemical responses.

To be healed we must withdraw our faith in all beliefs that lack compassion. Forgiveness is transformation that restores our natural neurochemical responses. The joy of young children is gradually depleted by the faith they place in educational and religious beliefs created to vicariously control their mind by programming it. MATTHEW 18:3 "*And said, Verily I say unto you, Except ye be converted, and become as little children, ye shall not enter into the kingdom of heaven.*" *The kingdom of heaven* is our whole mind. Our judgement is exiling us from heaven. Our salvation is the replacement of our beliefs with greater understanding.

When restored to our whole mind we are no longer victimised by the neurochemical responses of the body we inhabit. Forgiveness is the withdrawal of our faith in the beliefs that cause suffering to our self and others. After we realise our 'whole mind', our spirit and awareness exist in heaven and on earth. MATTHEW 6:10 KJV, "*Thy kingdom come, Thy will be done, on earth as it is in heaven*". Christ is the Christian saviour because without Christ there could be no Christianity. The Old Testament is not Christian. The second coming is the resurrection of our true identity which is the '*Christ-Self*' that our faith in our beliefs denies.

ROMANS 12:2 KJV *"And be not conformed to this world: but be ye transformed by the renewing of your mind, that ye may prove what is that good, and acceptable, and perfect, will of God."* A conditioned mind can only experience what it perceives to be experience. JOHN 2:15-17 KJV " *Love not the world, neither the things that are in the world. If any man love the world, the love of the Father is not in him. For all that is in the world, the lust of the flesh, and the lust of the eyes, and the pride of life, is not of the Father, but is of the world. And the world passeth away, and the lust thereof: but he that doeth the will of God abideth for ever.*"

Alpha and Omega

Everything exists within each one of us. We are each the 'alpha' and the 'omega' that represents the whole of creation which is the life existing in all things. We have each been told that we are a separate part of the whole of mankind existing as an individual. When we believe that we exist as an individual part of the whole we exist in perceived separation. The parts of the self we reject are reflected in others. In truth it is the perceived self that is separate and foreign. We each individually worship the 'one-entity' that is the 'I-entity' that is our identity.

War is like a body that rejects its own organs. The head can enter into a conflict with the heart until one or the other can no longer withstand the attack even though each needs the other for their continued existence. God is the whole that includes the separate parts of every single body and community. If the separated minds of people and communities live in conflict it is because they have rejected God. In each body this micro-conflict is experienced as disease and suffering that causes death. In the environment this conflict of the mind is experienced as the macro-conflict of war.

If there is balance within a mind and body, the sum parts work in service of the whole existing in a communion of mind, body and spirit. Separate parts have no value in and of themselves. If one perspective defines itself as separate or different from its own kind it may reject the others. The heart is not the mind and the mind is not the heart. Arjuna's compassion represents the heart that knew it should not fight the brain, kidneys or lungs but had to fight to protect the whole because like each cell in the body it was his function to fight for the whole if it was attacked by other parts.

As Krishna pointed out, if we do not play our part and serve when we must serve, the whole will not function. Krishna represents the 'whole' of everything, including each body, person and community. If just one part of the mind that controls the separate functions of the body can be persuaded to betray the whole mind in which it exists, that body cannot survive. Judas Iscariot is an example of what happens when one part separates itself from the whole. Any belief that is in conflict with another belief in the same mind creates conflict that destroys the believer with disease of mind and body.

Each belief that is in conflict with other beliefs within the whole mind is a 'sin'. ROMANS, KJV, 6:23, *"For the wages of sin is death; but the gift of God is eternal life through Jesus Christ our Lord."* It takes just one belief within a mind to cause the red face of embarrassment. It takes just one belief within the mind to cause the brain to reduce or cut the supply of blood and oxygen to the lungs, limbs and heart. When our mind is in conflict our body is under a constant attack that may take years to kill the believer.

It is the thoughts and feelings of a mind whose beliefs are in conflict that are the cause of suicide. Suicide is the body 'murdering' its own God and creator at the command of beliefs that the believer has put his/her

ALPHA AND OMEGA

mind's faith in without wisdom. Conflicting and selfish beliefs are sins which create fear, anxiety and suffering leading to sickness, disease and death. Christ is the whole mind of each child before its mind is conditioned to believe it is a separate child existing as an 'I-entity'. The 'I-entity' is a sin existing as the selfish identity.

The identity is installed by others to separate the child from its divinity creating division, duality and conflict within the same mind. Our sick minds have become separate parts of a whole world that is being deprived of the contribution of the parts that are essential for its continued existence. REVELATION 21:6, KJV, *"And he said unto me, It is done. I am Alpha and Omega, the beginning and the end. I will give unto him that is athirst of the fountain of the water of life freely."* All parts must live in harmony if the whole is to survive.

An antibody that kills a cell does so as a compassionate act to protect the healthy cells that serve the whole in an effort to remove conflict and prevent disease from destroying the body. If alien cells created by beliefs kill just one innocent cell it is as if they kill the whole body. If an antibody fights to save just one cell it is as if it is saves the whole world. Each individual mind is conditioned by education to perceive a world that is merely a projection of an inner world designed by beliefs that prejudice that mind's perception. All conflict is created within the mind.

The jihad takes place within the mind. In our insanity we pray for God to take sides in a battle between the heart and mind of a body that requires both for its existence. The atonement refers to the communion of the separated parts within the whole mind existing as the conflicting beliefs that persecute the believer. Atonement is the only way to fellowship and communion. For peace to return to the mind all conflicting beliefs within the mind must surrender to the believer that is their creator and God so they can be converted and saved. This is salvation.

Just two conflicting beliefs can cause and sustain poverty, disease and suffering. Life coaches develop strategies to overcome difficulties hallucinated within the mind. These difficulties are not inherent in the experience, but are believed to be inherent. Each individual mind can be liberated or incarcerated simply by their application of beliefs existing in the context of *I can* and/or *I can't*. MATHEW 18:19, KJV, "*Again I say unto you, That if two of you shall agree on earth as touching any thing that they shall ask, it shall be done for them of my Father which is in heaven.*"

An Incarcerated Mind

Our mind's freedom of expression is limited by our personal vocabulary. Our vocabulary determines the limits of our mind's ability to understand and express itself. If we believe we can do some things but not others those beliefs determine the limits of our mind's freedom of expression. Our beliefs incarcerate our mind within our own personal belief system. The most creative and successful people are perceived in this way because their creative expression is extraordinary and unique. So why aren't we all achieving what the most successful people are achieving?

Why aren't we all great musicians, artists, authors or inventors? It is accepted that each one of us is unique so why do most of us think and behave in generic terms? It is because we are each and all unique that we each have the same potential to express what is unique about 'us' surpassing the feats of the pioneers that came before us. There is only one of us and we each have a mind and a body, so why do some achieve extraordinary success whilst others do not? There are two things that determine how our unique creative potential is expressed. Those two things are -

1. How we perceive our self
2. How we perceive what is defined to be reality

How we perceive our self is defined by what we believe about our self. What I believe *I am* prejudices my perception of me and my ability. My perception of me is defined by the words I use to describe the self that I define to be 'me'. The only truth that is revealed by how we define our self is our beliefs and the limits of our personal voluntary expression. How each individual defines themselves in the context of 'I am' will determine what *I can* do. Within my mind, the limits of what I can do are enforced by what my mind believes I *cannot* do.

For example when describing myself
I may say '*I am not*'-

- *good looking*
- *smart*
- *intelligent*
- *confident*
- *outgoing*
- *fearless*
- *curious*
- *happy, or*
- *popular*

If I have put my mind's faith in these beliefs then my mind and body will not be able to comfortably engage in any activity that requires these qualities. The beliefs I create about what *I can* and what *I cannot* do define the parameters of my behavioural and creative expression. The beliefs in the context of *I am not* create and enforce limits within my mind that sustain constraints on who and what *I am*. If

An Incarcerated Mind

I encounter any situation that exceeds the limits of this self-programming I will feel discomfort, confusion and fear. When expressed these states of mind and body will usually be expressed using the phrase 'I cannot'.

How we perceive our self reflects what we believe about our self. What we believe about reality determines how we perceive reality. What defines how we perceive our self and our experience is determined by how we assemble the words of our personal vocabulary to create and sustain our personal belief system. Paradoxically, our unlimited mind is incarcerated and 'hypnotised' by the beliefs that we each place our faith in. A belief is not the believer's personal truth. Any belief that we place our minds faith in has the faith of God in it. This is why our beliefs have absolute power over us.

Many have not yet realised that our beliefs only have our power whilst they have our faith. We can only believe what we do not know because when we know we have no need of beliefs because *we know*. We are the believer, not the belief. Our beliefs need us but we need no beliefs to exist. The only way to transcend the limitations we feel is to question what we believe. Each one of our beliefs is not our truth. We don't need beliefs when we know. We can only believe what we do not know. There are no limits to our power but those our faith places upon our own unique personal expression. Any belief that has our faith usurps our mind's power with our own mind's power to control our mind.

There are two ways to clear our mind from the existential incarceration created in the moment we place our faith in beliefs that 'trespass' within our own mind

The first is to transform each and every application of the phrase *I cannot* into *I can*.

The second is to realise we are not 'who' we perceive our self to be. We are the believer who believed we were what we now define our own self to be.

To convert all the beliefs that exist in the context of *I cannot* into *I can* will transform our life. To convert all the examples of *I cannot* into *I can* will not enlighten the 'self' who believes, thinks and creates in such limited terms. To permanently escape limitation and allow the full creative expression of the whole mind requires our mind to be converted. The salvation of the self by the Christ within can only occur with the realisation that we cannot be defined, so we cannot be what our beliefs define our self to be. Perception is the effect of belief.

When the child believes in the identity assigned within the jurisdiction where it is born, it is usurped by its own faith. Unique creative expression is only incarcerated by generic beliefs about what we *can* and *cannot* do. Each mind's faith is placed in a generic identity. We have allowed our minds to be programmed by Judaism, Islam, Christianity and Hinduism which becomes the mind's criteria for what can be believed and what must be rejected. Religious beliefs place limitations where in truth there are no limitations.

As religions lose their power they are replaced by 'political philosophy'. Religions do not represent God and politicians do not represent the people.

Archetypes and the Mind

In all societies everyone is expected to create and play the part of a culturally compliant 'archetype' for their entire life. Archetypal data remains within the 'whole mind' after the body dies. Our faith allows archetypes to take our place within our own mind. All societies expect each child to deny their own true self. Archetypes can be fictional like Tarzan or Sherlock Holmes or real people. Jesus is an Archetypal Christian and Muhammad is an archetypal Muslim. Political figures such as Mandela, Hitler and Stalin are held up as political archetypes that personify good and evil.

What has our faith controls our mind. What has our faith is our beliefs. Our unlimited mind is expressed as the life in our body. Only our faith can keep our mind incarcerated within existential parameters sustained *exclusively* by our beliefs. Every moment of every life from the moment of each body's birth until its death is recorded as data within the whole mind. Each body's 'life-record' commences when consciousness enters the body and continues until consciousness leaves the body. Denial of our deeds in life cannot remove those records from the whole mind.

The unique record of every moment of every life is stored within the whole mind. The mind is not within the brain. The brain evolves to operate the body. The mind is not within the brain's cellular structure. The cells serve the mind that operates the body. Our experience evolves our understanding. *Before language* the cells inherited functions passed down. This is currently defined to be genetic determinism. The whole mind has the power to edit our cellular expression. The editing of cellular function evolves, disrupts and attacks our body's functions and those of our offspring.

What has our faith controls our mind. Faith is the exclusive cause of all stress related sickness and chronic disease. Genetically inherited disease is caused by the beliefs of the parents editing cells that are passed to their children. Illness caused by genetic inheritance is not God's punishment, it is the legacy of the judgement of our ancestors. Every moment of every creature that ever lived is recorded within the whole mind. The body does not have a 'personal mind' but its abode within the whole mind is called the soul. The body is the medium for a soul's life on earth.

The whole mind's power is harnessed by those who persuade the soul that it is the body in which its conscious awareness dwells. Any word or concept that defines what God created is bearing false witness. It is God's faith that is obtained when the innocent child believes it is *who* it is told it is. The child's faith is God's faith. This faith in the identity is how the child's divinity becomes incarcerated within the perspective of an identity created on earth. God's faith in the beliefs of each child allows demons to enter and trespass within the mind disguised as personal beliefs.

What does this mean? It means that everything and everyone is sustained by the unlimited power and understanding of the whole mind of God. All the information and experiences of all that are alive now and

ARCHEYTYPES AND THE MIND

all that came before are stored within the whole mind. *We all exist within the whole mind* We each and all have equal access to everything that is contained within the whole mind. We only live in limitation because our whole mind's faith in limiting beliefs is a denial, refusal and rejection of a *greater understanding*.

Dogmatic faith denies any greater understanding. There are no problems in the world. What is defined as a problem is the effect of limiting beliefs. Each perspective has the power to create or destroy. Those who place their faith in archetypal beliefs call on archetypal forces to possess and control their mind. When we believe in the words of an archetype, that archetype is reborn again in us and possesses our mind. If we place our faith in the beliefs of Alexander, Jesus, Ghandi, Machiavelli, Hitler, Stalin or Dr. Martin Luther King they are *born again* in us.

It was our faith in archetypal beliefs that gave those beliefs our authority to take our place within our own mind. With our faith our beliefs control what we think and feel. Many placed their faith in Hitler's words not realising he was resurrecting *demonic archetypes* that would take control of his mind. Only our faith can allow demonic concepts to possess our mind and body. Jesus is born again in us when we place our faith in the words of Jesus. When will Jesus return? Jesus returns to save each one of us when we place our faith in the words of Jesus.

A mind that cannot kill *cannot kill*. Placing our faith in the words of Jesus ensures we *cannot* kill. A phobia demonstrates the power that all beliefs have over the mind. War results from placing our faith in a belief that justifies killing allowing demonic archetypal killers to possess our mind. The 'authorities' of the earth use education to program the whole mind through the eyes and ears of all children. Only a child's faith in limitation inhibits the unlimited power of the whole mind's creative expression. Beliefs cannot be installed into the whole mind without faith.

Faith is the most powerful thing in existence. Our faith is all that is required for others to install beliefs into the mind that sustains us. Education ensures that we collectively believe in a generically perceived reality. To control the whole mind's unique bodily expression we obtain a believer's faith in concepts that limit personal expression. Patriotism is the concept used to ensure that we kill for our country. What has our faith determines if are possessed by creative, wise, compassionate and peaceful archetypes or selfish, evil and violent 'demonic' archetypes.

Our faith in demonic beliefs allows archetypal demons to enter, dwell and to take our place to control our *unlimited mind*. Some share the beliefs of Hitler, Vlad III, Stalin and Alexander. Some share the beliefs of Buddha, Christ, Krishna and Muhammad. Only our faith permits archetypes to take up residence with the whole mind that controls our mind and body. Faith calls on unlimited archetypal forces that can create or destroy. The beliefs that have our mind's faith can be angelic or demonic. Our faith alone gives these demonic archetypes our authority to enter our mind.

When we no longer wish to be an addict, victim or victimiser, these archetypes become trespassers that we fight to suppress. God is the greater understanding that exists *beyond all understanding.* This is why God is our only salvation. Our faith in the beliefs installed by others gave archetypal rapists, murderers, addicts and fearful victims the authority to possess our mind to take control over our body to use it for sin. Forgiveness is the withdrawal of our faith in any beliefs that lack compassion. When we withdraw our faith in beliefs that lack compassion we are free.

We are our own saviours. We haven't all realised yet that we are what we have been waiting for. The second coming of Christ refers to us. This is why we forgive. We forgive those beliefs that trespass against us because without our faith those beliefs could not have entered our mind. Forgive is an English word that was not in the original text of the Bible. The Aramaic word is *shbag* which means 'to cancel, to let loose, or to untie'. We untie ourselves from the contracts we enter into when we place our faith in beliefs. *Shbag* means to withdraw our faith in beliefs.

We free our heart and mind by the withdrawal of our faith in demonic beliefs. Our forgiveness is our salvation. Our faith is the most powerful thing in existence. MATTHEW 17:20, KJV *"And Jesus said unto them, Because of your unbelief: for verily I say unto you, If ye have faith as a grain of mustard seed, ye shall say unto this mountain, Remove hence to yonder place; and it shall remove; and nothing shall be impossible unto you"*. If we believe *we can't,* then in our mind *we can't.* If we withdraw our faith in this belief we are no longer incarcerated within this limitation.

Eventually we will all realise that the words

of Christ were truth. The whole mind is heaven. Only beliefs installed within our whole mind by others through our eyes and ears can trespass in our place exiling us from heaven. LUKE 11:2, KJV "*And he said unto them, When ye pray, say, Our Father which art in heaven, Hallowed be thy name. Thy kingdom come. Thy will be done, as in heaven, so in earth.*" Beliefs are 'sins'. LUKE 11:2, KJV "*And forgive us our sins; for we also forgive every one that is indebted to us. And lead us not into temptation; but deliver us from evil.*"

A priest, monk, nun, politician, policeman, sportsman, worker, leader, soldier, American, European, Arab, Christian, Muslim, Jew, doctor, nurse, criminal or gang member are archetypes. Each of those archetypal existences is sustained by beliefs. To transcend the control any belief has over our mind we simply withdraw our faith in it. What we believe about our self we become. All beliefs are prayers. All prayers are always answered. To ask God to give you a different life or make you happy is not a prayer. *Our life is our prayers answered in full.* Our beliefs are our prayers.

What we believe we create. If we can be persuaded to believe in 'demonic concepts' those concepts are prayers that admit trespassers into our mind. If we place our faith in beliefs that justify hating Muslims, Americans, Christians or Jews, then all we need to do is think about or encounter someone who conforms to those archetypes and our chemistry will respond with feelings of hatred and enmity. Once a belief has our faith, those beliefs control our thoughts, words and behaviour. We are each and all unique expressions of the consciousness that manifests as life. *We are not archetypes.*

Comfort Zone and Addiction

Each mind uses fear to guard the boundary of its personal comfort zone. We cannot leave our personal comfort zone without facing what we fear. The comfort zone is sustained by beliefs about what lies beyond it. If we contemplate moving beyond our personal comfort zone our mind will focus on the fears we created our comfort zone to avoid. Fear is the jailor of our mind. Fear ensures we never escape the existential parameters of our personal comfort zone. The zone which is a personal prison is only comfortable by comparison with our fear of what lies beyond.

What is commonly referred to as the comfort zone is the personal prison. The comfort zone establishes the existential parameters within which we individually feel comfortable and beyond which we do not. Each mind is programmed by its beliefs to fear what lies beyond its personal comfort zone. At some point the comfort zone becomes uncomfortable and the individual may wish to leave or escape it. With each failed attempt to overcome the fear that prevents any comfortable attempts to exist outside our personal comfort zone we gradually begin to dislike our life and our self.

Many do not realise that they exist within the existential parameters of a prison that is enforced by their own mind's self-programming. Each mind is programmed by beliefs which establish the parameters of voluntary self-expression. People compromise and settle for the best available within the limits of their personal comfort zone in many areas, aspects and contexts. As this occurs life can begin to feel repetitive, boring, unfulfilled, unhappy or unbearable. When a person is no longer content with their life but fears what lies beyond their comfort zone, they can feel helpless.

Our frustration with life is caused by our mind's faith in beliefs that exist in the context of *I can't*. An incarcerated mind sees very few options to remedy or alleviate this condition. There is however one universal strategy that an incarcerated mind uses to temporarily escape the effects of its own self-incarceration. It is both legal and illegal and is exploited by industry and crime. The way to temporarily escape the limited feelings of the personal comfort zone is through exposure to any addictive stimulus that allows us to feel more comfortable or better.

Most of the world has become addicted because of a life unfulfilled. The unfulfilled life is caused by our mind's faith in fearful beliefs which control our thought and feelings when we think about or are exposed to what our beliefs fear. The way to transcend the limits of a personal comfort zone is to remove the limits that sustain it. What sustains our personal comfort zone is what we believe about what lies beyond it. Fear is the body's chemical response to what our mind believes about what lies beyond our personal comfort zone.

If I no longer believe that there is risk or danger in a particular endeavour then I can feel no discomfort when I participate in that endeavour. We can fear talking to people. We can fear activities. We may wish that

Comfort Zone and Addiction

we could participate in what lies beyond our comfort zone but are controlled by what may be conscious or unconscious beliefs. Beliefs are the universal cause of the chemical effect that is generically defined using the term 'fear'. Exposure to addictive stimulus creates temporary access to the feelings that lie beyond our personal comfort zone without leaving it.

The drugs, alcohol and tobacco industries are evidence that most people in the world transcend the lower vibration (feelings) caused by remaining within their personal comfort zone by exposure to the addictive stimulus that creates a 'higher' vibration. To permanently escape we must find out what prevents our escape. We must face and investigate the truth of why we fear what we fear. The cause of fear is always a belief that prevents voluntary self-expression. It is only by withdrawing our faith in beliefs that sustain our comfort zone that we can expand it.

Conditioned Responses

Our personal definitions for 'good' and 'bad' create our personal tolerances and intolerances. When we individually define what is good and what is bad we condition our personal responses to any stimulus that conforms to one of those contrasting definitions. Our mind's individual conditioning is the cause of what we perceive to be our 'good days' and our 'bad days'. Our personal prejudices condition our behavioural and emotional responses. We deliberately create conditioned behavioural responses in order to avoid being fully present when undertaking mundane repetitive activities.

When showering, getting dressed, typing or driving our car, our mind's conditioning takes the place of our full awareness. In long standing relationships two people can hold conversations without really listening or being fully present. When we condition our mind, our mind becomes the shepherd and we become the sheep. When driving a car we may consciously decide to turn right or left but we leave the operating of the vehicle to our 'conditioned responses'. The mind is ever vigilant of our seen experience and its reactions are instant. If a pedestrian walks into the path of our vehicle our mind's full awareness takes control.

The conditioning of our own mind can be spontaneous and unconscious. For example if we get a kick to the shin bone the pain we experience from one single

Conditioned Responses

kick to this area can be enough to create a conditioned response that ensures our body avoids situations that may result in the same pain for our entire life. This natural ability ensures we can avoid pain. When discovered this phenomenon was used by others to install conditioned responses into our mind in order to control us. The conditioning of a child's behaviour was once referred to as 'teaching him manners'. Manners are conditioned behavioural responses.

In history a Christian child that did not exhibit the correct behavioural responses was considered to be a sinner or to lack manners. Therefore bad mannered children were beaten to create conditioned responses to prevent the expression of any behaviour that was prohibited. It is the influence or control of family, religion, education and peer groups that condition a child's mind. Professional boxers, footballers, bricklayers and welders develop conditioned behavioural responses that achieve consistent results. These behaviours are defined as 'skills'. Conditioned responses are not limited to productive behavioural responses.

There are also conditioned responses that are violent and criminal. An army trains its recruits to exhibit the appropriate conditioned responses to be activated on command. A conditioned response can win us a medal in sport. A conditioned response of violence can win us a medal in war. A violent conditioned response in times of peace can result in imprisonment. Some conditioned responses can result in a loss of friendships and a breakdown of a marriage. Once they are created our conditioned responses can work below our conscious awareness and we may feel unable to change.

A phobia is a conditioned response. A phobia can result from one single experience. A dog bite, a violent attack or a rape can create debilitating conditioned responses. A phobia is created by our mind to protect us by avoiding certain experiences. Phobic conditioned responses are created by our belief that similar or qualifying situations will result in a specific outcome or that they contain risk. If we decide we no longer wish to face a risk our mind may create a fearful response or phobia. Whilst phobic conditioned responses are debilitating they are created as resources by our own mind to protect us.

To acquire and retain particular skills we practice our behaviour until we are satisfied that we have developed a sufficient level of skill. This is how we design and create behaviourally induced conditioned responses that we refer to as 'skills'. We learn a skill by repeating a behaviour until the variances in our results do not affect our ability to achieve the desired objective. For example, a footballer may spend hours, days or weeks perfecting his penalty taking skills until he can achieve consistent results without any conscious effort. When being trained to drive we are taught to check our mirrors before signalling and then manoeuvring.

Most drivers can drive a vehicle at high speed with little or no conscious effort, holding conversations and listening to the radio whilst looking at the scenery. Whilst a conditioned response can be a resource in one context it can become a limitation in another. A phobia is nothing more than a conditioned response. Conditioned responses can be both debilitating and liberating. If we look around the world we see examples of what we may define as 'good' and 'bad' conditioned responses. For example, we may define the conditioned responses of a racing driver, martial artist, a guitar player or aircraft stunt pilot to be amazing.

The world contains many examples of conditioned responses that are destructive such as a riots, terrorism, violence, rape, provocative statements and loss of temper. The context of certain behaviours such as sports like martial arts and boxing are acceptable because of the voluntary participation of competitors. To voluntarily engage in wars that injure, maim, rape and destroy whole communities and countries is also considered to be acceptable by those who plan and execute those activities. In most parts of the world the minds of Christians and Muslims are pre-conditioned so that they can be persuaded to kill.

When recruits enter basic training for the armed forces they are quickly conditioned to deny their own natural reactions. Our natural reaction is compassion. The will of each recruit must surrender in order to develop the conditioned responses that are necessary to ensure they deny their own compassion to kill what God created. The conditioning of the mind of mankind means that each child is born into an existential paradigm that is the collective belief systems sustained only by their parent's faith. We are each a vehicle for the conscious expression of the unlimited creative force that sustains all life.

We are the believer spoken about in scriptures. Our faith determines how our creative expression is manifested in this life. Whatever has our mind's faith will be expressed by us. Those who benefit from what has our collective mind's faith want to retain control over what we believe. There are no limits to our individual creative expression. We only exist in perceived limitation whilst we sustain our faith in limitation. We create fixed responses to any stimulus simply by defining it. How an experience feels depends on how we perceive it. Good and bad are concepts that reflect how we define our self and our experiences.

Religious conversion refers to a conversion of the mind. The conversion of our mind is essential if we are to free ourselves from the limitations that constrain it. Those limitations are the beliefs that use the power of an unlimited mind to constrain an unlimited mind. The power of an unlimited mind is faith. The mind cannot exceed what has the believer's faith. We are the believer. When we transcend our conditioned responses we realise the gifts of our unique expression. The only way to remove all limitations is to convert our mind. We convert our mind by withdrawing our faith in all beliefs that lack compassion.

Conviction

If our mind can imagine the most compelling, easy, enjoyable and rewarding path it will be something we can achieve with very little effort. If we look for success and happiness outside of our self in what we perceive to be reality without creating it within our mind we can find this only by the grace of God. If we create a compelling, enjoyable and easy existence within our minds then we can create it in our experience. Until we are comfortable doing something within our mind, we cannot be comfortable realising it in the world of experience. Every successful idea begins in the mind.

All great ideas and inventions began in the mind. If there is any cognitive dissonance then there is an issue within the mind. Until we are fully aligned with any path or endeavour there may be issues, dislikes or difficulties that interfere with the smooth transition from idea to experience. The mind and body must be in perfect harmony if the inner experience of the mind is to be translated into experience in the material world. Conviction means an individual knows with all their heart and mind that what they are seeing in their mind's eye is real and will come to pass.

With absolute conviction success is inevitable. Even our perceived failures demonstrate the power and success of a mind that was convinced it would fail. Our perceived success or failure results from a mind that was convinced it would succeed or fail. Conviction is unshakable faith that is beyond logic. Conviction is to know and be convinced of something within the mind requiring no independent evidence. Success or failure is pre-determined within the mind. Each mind is beyond measurement and 'never fails to achieve what it believes and envisions.

All of us have successfully created the life we are living. All of us have been 100% successful in realising the life created within our mind. If we take the life that our mind has created and compare it with external standards or people, we may judge it to be unworthy, unfulfilled or even unhappy. Regardless of how we judge our life or our accomplishments, we are living the life that our faith created. Our experience is the effect and what we put our minds faith in is the cause. Our faith in *I can't* is a prayer to an omnipotent mind that is always fulfilled in experience.

The limits of what we can do are enforced by what we *cannot* do. In truth there is nothing we cannot do. The paradox is that our mind has the power to believe and enforce parameters that limit the mind's creative expression. These boundaries are enforced by how we apply an instruction that programmes and limits the mind. The limits of our mind's expression are defined by the words that follow *I cannot*. I cannot is usually simplified to *I can't* in the English language. I can't speak in public. I can't think. I can't understand. I can't do this. I can't do that.

I can't is how the self limits its own mind's creative expression. We are limitless. To define the self is to place limits upon what is limitless. Paradoxically, the mind's faith in beliefs uses the mind's own power to programme and control the mind. The way to transcend the limits of the mind

CONVICTION

is to withdraw our faith in any belief that limits it. HEBREWS 11:1, KJV, *"Now faith is the substance of things hoped for, the evidence of things not seen."* When our faith is placed in beliefs that exist in the context of *I cannot* this prayer is always answered. Each life is a testimony of faith.

Our beliefs are a testimony to our mind's faith. MATTHEW 17:20, KJV, *"And Jesus said unto them, Because of your unbelief: for verily I say unto you, If ye have faith as a grain of mustard seed, ye shall say unto this mountain, Remove hence to yonder place; and it shall remove; and nothing shall be impossible unto you."* We have mistaken our mind's ability to consistently fail as a failure or inability. Our life is a testament to the power of our mind and our faith. JOB 11.8, KJV, *"It is as high as heaven; what canst thou do? deeper than hell; what canst thou know?"*

The perceived world and the perceived self is a 'reflection' of our mind's faith. If we change the beliefs that we have placed our mind's faith in we change our self and the world is transformed. When we say *I can't*, how do we know? Paradoxically we are the creator and product of our own mind. If we define what we cannot do before we even attempt to do it, this constraint can only be lifted by withdrawing our faith in that belief or conviction. Our greatest challenges are not to be found in experience. The greatest challenge is to free our self by removing our mind's faith in limiting beliefs.

Crime and Poverty

Crime is not the way out of poverty. Poverty is caused by the mind's faith. To live a life of crime is to live a life of chance. The mind expresses itself through the body's behaviour. When we commit crime we put our body's health and freedom of expression at risk. There are no signs showing us where the karmic traps lay. To create the wealth in experience we must first discover the wealth that is within us. To discover love in the world we must discover the love within us. To conquer the world and its temptations the seeker must realise that it is our own self we seek.

When we discover the true self we discover the unlimited creative source from which all life springs. When we discover the self we realise the self is our mind. It does not matter if our body is born into poverty or wealth. It is within our mind that our fortunes are won and lost. Within our mind we may be the most desperate among men or the happiest, richest and most successful. Our mind's faith determines whether we acquire, lose or regain wealth. Our unlimited mind can only be usurped by what we put our mind's faith in. To exist in poverty or wealth is to live without balance.

A life without balance is the fruit of a mind that lacks compassion. Without compassion the believer suffers. Poverty results from a mind that deprives the 'self' by worshipping a belief that their true identity is a self that lacks. Within each mind is peace, joy, happiness, poverty, unhappiness and pain. Which experience we experience is determined by the beliefs we place our mind's faith in. Poverty or abundance is a choice. As the poor will testify, their faith in beliefs that define the self as incapable, lacking or undeserving is a prayer that is always answered.

I cannot is a prayer and an instruction from the believer to his own mind. The belief *I cannot* creates a life of limitation and struggle. A believer whose beliefs lack wisdom becomes the victim of his own mind's power not realising that his mind's faith is using his own power to incarcerate him. Beliefs that enforce *I cannot* are the cause and creator of all mind-made limitations. The quality of all experience is how it feels. All feelings are created within our mind. The belief 'I cannot be happy' checkmates the believer's mind preventing happiness.

The paradox is that our beliefs are so powerful they can render us powerless in the moment we give our mind's faith to any belief that says I am powerless. The story of Samson and Delilah is the story of the power of the minds faith and the power of beliefs. Samson believed his power was caused by his hair and his mind's faith in this belief was powerful enough to make him powerless when his hair was cut. He lost no power when his hair was cut. His faith had just placed conditions upon its expression. The mind has the power to render itself impotent by empowering opposing beliefs.

The mind requires no beliefs but a believer does. The mind in each child believes it is what it is told it is by those who greet it. The mind enters the world through the body of each new born child. The belief that Samson's mind held about his hair created great strength but it also created a condition within his mind which had to be met before the mind's power could be expressed as the body's strength. His salvation came when he withdrew his faith in such limiting beliefs about the source of his power which led to the *greater understanding* that can only come from God.

A mind that is controlled by beliefs is not free. The mind's experience cannot exceed the mind's faith because the mind's power is its faith. Any belief existing within the mind in the context of *I cannot* is covertly concealing the unlimited power it constrains. If our mind attempts to dilute the power of *I cannot* by creating beliefs in the context of *I can* it will create conflict and confusion within the same mind. This kind of belief system results in an existential checkmate that incarcerates the believer within a domain commonly referred to as the comfort zone.

Conflicting beliefs mean we are playing the role of a gambler betting on two competing hands of cards in the same game. Each hand represents one set of beliefs that are in conflict with the other. We can only realise abundance by withdrawing our mind's faith in all beliefs that exist in the context of *I cannot*. The withdrawal of our faith removes the veil of perception sustained by beliefs that hold the innocent child's omnipotent mind hostage. The veil prevents the *second coming* that enables the omnipotent mind of the child to free itself from existential incarceration.

To be 'born again' is the realisation of the true self.

CRIME AND POVERTY

MATTHEW 18:3, KJV: *"And said, Verily I say unto you, Except ye be converted, and become as little children, ye shall not enter into the kingdom of heaven."* Our mind is the creator of our experience.

MARK 8:36, KJV: *"For what shall it profit a man, if he shall gain the whole world, and lose his own soul?"* We can only live in poverty if we live in 'denial' of God. What is God? God is the *greater understanding* that exists beyond all the beliefs that were created to define what we perceive to be the self and reality.

Poverty and unhappiness are sustained only for as long as our collective mind's faith is placed in beliefs that sustain and create those realities. The hypothesis is our understanding according to the words the mind uses as its witness. What our mind observes is prejudiced by what our mind believes. We believe that each word in the dictionary is what it represents. We have incarcerated our unlimited mind within the jurisdiction of a vocabulary. We existed before language. We have programmed our minds with language and our wisdom is now limited by what we believe.

We can only believe what we do not know. Each belief that has our minds faith is given control over our mind and body. Our voluntary personal expression cannot exceed our mind's beliefs as long as those beliefs have our mind's faith. Each belief about the self sows a seed in the mind of the believer that always comes to fruition when germinated by experience. Our ideas are our creative potential and our faith is the catalyst for converting ideas into personal experience. We must sow the seed of faith if we are to bring our full creative expression into existence.

What is the self? The self is a unique perspective

that is equal to all other perspectives. Therefore any definition that separates the self from others is not true. The only thing that can prevent our mind creating and becoming aware of ideas is our mind's faith and allegiance to conflicting and/or limiting beliefs. If I believe I cannot become successful I have given my mind's allegiance to the seed of this prayer and because it has the power of my fertile mind, my mind will deliver the limited thoughts and feelings that ensure I never become successful.

A life of poverty, crime and incarceration is proof of the power of faith, prayer and God. Only by withdrawing our faith in our beliefs can our mind realise *greater understanding*. God is the greater understanding that exists beyond all beliefs, hypotheses and concepts that define what is real and possible. The concepts of 'history' and 'archaeology' show us that the possibilities are limitless but the beliefs that constrain creative expression are not. A criminal is a mind that has become a victim of beliefs that define the self and others to be unworthy of compassion.

Compassion is the feelings of others which we put above the feelings of the self. When compassion is restored to the mind it is not possible to attack, rape, rob or kill.

Demons

Each time we give our mind's allegiance to any belief we contaminate, replace and revise the mind that existed before we put its faith in that belief. The mind of each believer is controlled by its beliefs for the period that they have the mind's faith. Our life is the effect of our mind's faith. God creates us. Our mind creates our experience. To become a plumber, architect, chef, engineer, soldier or criminal requires particular beliefs. Our mind is unlimited but our faith gives us power over it. We are God's creation. The faith we place in beliefs gives them power over our mind.

Each mind's programming is replaced and revised with each belief the mind acquires about the self. We are gradually replaced by our judgement existing in the form of our mind's ever increasing number of beliefs. What we believe has the power of our own mind. We are the mind. Our creative expression can only be inhibited or prevented by beliefs. Evil beliefs can force a 'good man' to become a 'bad man'. Beliefs are what can change 'peace' into 'war' and 'marriage' into 'divorce'. In our insanity we can look in the mirror at what God created and judge it to be unworthy.

We are each encouraged to create an archetype in our own imagination that we then work to become. This archetype requires us to first believe we can become what it is we aspire to become. Over a lifetime we acquire thousands of beliefs creating thousands of archetypal revisions of the self that exist within the mind like a

Russian Matryoshka doll. Each separate belief about the self creates a revised 'archetypal' me that competes with other conflicting archetypes for their continued existence within the mind. The first archetype is the identity installed within the mind of each child.

When the mind demonstrates conformance with the official archetype of the identity a 'me' perspective is created. The beliefs of this *me perspective* usurp and supersede the believer. The objective of each belief is to prejudice the mind's perception in order to control the believer. A belief replaces the mind's autonomy and impartiality with prejudices that control perception. Beliefs about the self we once called demons. The beliefs multiply to collectively create an abode for the *ego*, once called the devil. As each belief about the self is acquired the child's mind is gradually replaced.

Man is always at the mercy of the mind of his given identity which aspires to become an archetype. All beliefs prejudice the mind's perception to replace reality with a perceived reality. With our faith, our beliefs have become our mind's God. If I believe I cannot fight, then I cannot fight. If I believe I can and also believe that I cannot, I cannot easily. If I believe I would make a good doctor but also believe I am not intelligent enough to pass the exams, I create a conflict within my mind. In this example there are two demons within me, each fighting for control of my mind.

Demons fight within us because without our faith in the beliefs that sustain them they no longer exist within our mind. There are 'addiction' demons that rely upon beliefs to constrain our creative expression, compelling us to escape our comfort zone through exposure to the addictive stimulus. 'Conflict' demons are represented by concepts such as 'terrorism', 'security', 'enemy', 'blasphemy', 'justification' and 'democracy'. Conceptual demons wait until our mind can be tempted to place our faith in them. The mind's faith in demonic concepts gives those concepts control of over our mind.

The demon of 'addiction' has a legion under its command. Demons take possession of our mind and body through our exposure to alcohol, drugs, anger, sex and food. We are not addicted. We are incarcerated within limitations which are enforced by *demonic* beliefs. These demons wait for the mind to be in the most vulnerable or impressionable state. If our mind puts its faith in concepts we give those concepts permission to move in and take possession and control of our mind. The prayer and belief of a devotee of the demon of addiction is the belief *I can't stop.*

Beliefs are prayers that are always answered. If a demon can disguise itself as a concept that the mind can be educated to put its faith in it will control that mind for as long as it has that mind's faith. As innocent children our minds are susceptible to the influence and manipulation of others. If we believe the words of others, those words become beliefs within our mind. Religion, media, advertising and marketing are the common mediums of demonic influence. Those professions are rewarded with money for creating 'devotees' of believers.

There are 'success' and 'wealth' demons that reward those who manipulate the many for the benefit of a few. In religion, the exorcism was done to remove the cause of the behaviour considered to be demonic. The cause of the behaviour is the beliefs that justify that behaviour. Justification is a demon that masquerades as 'justice' in order to justify killing. 'Thou shalt not kill' is overruled by demonic beliefs that tempt the righteous to deny their own compassion. Compassion is not a concept it is our natural state. When compassion is restored we cannot do the bidding of demons.

We only need to withdraw our mind's faith in any belief to remove its power over our mind. We can only believe what we do not know because when we know we have no need of beliefs *because we know*. JAMES 8:32, KJV, "*And ye shall know the truth, and the truth shall make you free.*" We are forgiven for we have never killed. EXODUS 20:13, KJV, *"thou shalt not kill"* means we could not kill. What we believed allowed a demon to enter our mind to control it and use our body for 'sin'. Demonic beliefs control our mind for sin in the same way software controls a computer.

When society incarcerates these demons in prisons they also incarcerate the hostage in whose mind they exist. Their hostage is the innocent child whose mind was infiltrated by beliefs. Man's salvation or condemnation is determined by his beliefs. We exorcise demons when we withdraw our faith in beliefs that lack compassion. From childhood demons enter the mind within beliefs acquired over a lifetime. MATTHEW 18:2, KJV, "*And said, Verily I say unto you, Except ye be converted, and become as little children, ye shall not enter into the kingdom of heaven.*"

Do Unto Others

If we have compassion we can do no harm to others unless it is a compassionate act to protect the self or others. For many the meaning of LUKE 6:31, KJV, "*And as ye would that men should do to you, do ye also to them likewise*" is about treating others as we would have them treat us. There are preachers who say treat others as well as you would have them treat you. What is not mentioned is compassion. With compassion 'demons' cannot enter the mind to use the body to commit rape, robbery, attacks and murders. When a rapist rapes, there are two victims.

When a rapist is raping his victim he is also being raped by the demon that creates false desire triggering chemical reactions of arousal within the body of the rapist to compel the rapist to rape. When we attack we allow a demonic concept to justify the denial of our own compassion. Justification is how we can deny our own compassion. Compassion is our eternal connection with the source of the feelings that exist in all living creatures. When we attack, we are also being violently attacked but our attacker cannot be seen because our attacker is *within* our own mind.

The attack we inflict upon others is an attack upon the one eternal self that exists within all living creatures. This self is the source of life itself. We are not our name, nationality or religious identity. The truth of us in each moment is the awareness expressed through our behaviour. This is why there is forgiveness. We are our behaviour, so it does not matter if we are Christian, Muslim, Jew, Arab, American or European. If your faith means you go to a church, mosque or synagogue but you are a rapist or a murderer then it is not your religious faith but your deeds that define you.

When we live in service to others we live in service to God and uphold the scriptures. If we live in service to others our behaviour and our transgressions are forgiven because the truth of us is our behaviour, not our words, religion or testimony. When we allow beliefs, thoughts and feelings to enter our mind and body that lack compassion we allow 'demons' to enter our mind to seduce or torment us by controlling our thoughts, feelings and behaviour. When we feel anything that feels bad we should question our mind's explanation for why we feel bad.

Our mind justifies our own victimisation by disturbing our peace of mind with recurring thoughts and feelings. Justification is a 'demon' that masquerades as 'justice'. There is no justification for an act that lacks compassion. If we wish to attack others because they have attacked us then we have misunderstood because truth is not about retaliation, vengeance or revenge. Each innocent child is trespassed against by the beliefs of the educated mind their identity. Education programmes and conditions the mind to overwrite compassion with other more appropriate reactions.

Everyone we meet is a hostage and their beliefs are the jailors of their conditioned mind. If we observed an innocent child from birth we would gradually change our perception of that child as the child grows into an adult. The innocent child's mind is incarcerated by programming and conditioning. Each mind is conditioned by others who use language to install meaning. Everyone else is reflecting our mind's 'tolerance'. Our anxious, fearful or angry responses toward others reflect the limits of our mind's tolerance demonstrated by our intolerance of their words and behaviour.

The people we accept without judgement are those that the personal prejudices of our mind can tolerate. The people we criticise and object to reveal the personal limits of our mind's tolerance. The limit of our tolerance is the threshold beyond which we attack our own mind and body with particular thoughts and feelings. If we can justify an attack on those we cannot tolerate then we may also attack them. Our rejection of others is a rejection of the same part existing within our self as a concept. What we are rejecting is the parts within our self we have denied, condemned and rejected.

Each person we reject is revealing the part of us we are denying within our self. Our mind can only perceive what our mind's faith is *devoted to*. To perceive an 'unbeliever' we must allow the concept of an 'unbeliever' to enter and trespass within our mind to control our mind's perception. In order to conceal its control over the believer, the concept 'unbeliever' points the finger at others to conceal the fact that *we are worshipping it* as a concept. The unbeliever is within. If the unbeliever were not within it would be impossible for our mind to detect it.

All concepts that cause or justify suffering are demonic. All demonic concepts were created to disturb the mind causing pain, suffering and death. All a demonic concept requires to gain entry into our mind is our faith in it. We reject the truth that lays beneath the judgemental concepts our mind projects to define others. So if I say I hate Christians because they are 'non-believers', then my mind's belief harbours and worships a 'non-believer'. Each mind worships and is controlled and programmed by its own beliefs. Everyone that accepts their 'given name' is a believer.

We must believe our given name is who we are before we can become this. This means that we all believers. Who we believe we are is a trespasser. The identity is a trespasser that is placed within our mind by others. It is the 'trespasser' that is the unbeliever or false self. The unbeliever is the perspective of the identity and the believer is the child that was 'trespassed' against with this false witness who we each believe is the whole of who and what we are. This means that until we realise, we are each and all the 'believer' and the 'unbeliever'.

This also means that the jihad is within, not without. We cannot defeat an enemy that is within by looking for him in others. Regardless of our situation we cannot hold others to be responsible for what we think and feel. Those who persuade others to leave their home and family to kill and destroy in the name of God have been deceived by the devil. The devil can only live in the mind of man. The devil requires our faith in a separate identity before it can use this belief as the vehicle to enter and take control of the mind of the believer. The given 'identity' is the 'devil'.

The devil cannot enter the mind without the mind's faith. Our faith in our given identity permits

Do Unto Others

this 'trespasser' to enter our mind to take our place. The devil is the unbeliever usurping us to take our place. Only a devil could justify killing, rape, enslavement and destruction. *We are our behaviour*! We believed we were who were told were because we did not know. Luke 23:24, KJV, *"Then said Jesus, Father, forgive them; for they know not what they do". Luke 6:14, KJV, "For if ye forgive men their trespasses, your heavenly Father will also forgive you."*

Duality and Non-Duality

The *ego* mind is our whole mind's awareness confined within the parameters of an identity. The fixed perspective of the identity confines the awareness of each unique 'body' to the 'body's' unique perspective. If we remained as those in the animal kingdom our individual behavioural expression would be limited to generics. The perceived 'duality' is created when our parents install a *who* perspective (name) that is conditioned and programmed with beliefs. If language doesn't condition the child's mind the child is perceived to be abnormal, psychotic or mentally handicapped.

The 'whole mind' cannot be educated because the whole mind is the non-local collective mind of mankind. The whole collective mind is the single source of each individual perspective. If we could educate the one whole mind in which the separate perspectives of each separate identity exist then that whole (non-dual) mind would have been incarcerated by dogmatic beliefs thousands of years ago. Duality is required if there is to be a separate mind for each 'perspective' that can evolve in technological terms. To create technology we required a separate critical perspective.

The perceived duality is the creator and his creation. Only a separate individual perspective can judge what God created to be less than what it should be. The duality between the whole mind and the mind of the identity is necessary to create the hypotheses

Duality and Non-Duality

that question *what is*. Conceptual criteria enabled the mind to establish a benchmark or 'archetype' that was be used to judge people and things. Hypotheses were developed to question whether standards could be improved to achieve goals. It is man's judgement that was the creator of technological evolution.

The end of duality is the end of each man's freedom to individually express his unique creative potential. If we existed as the animals, insects, birds and fishes do, it would only be our environment that influenced how man evolved. With a judgemental mind we can make ourselves feel bored, scared, critical, suspicious, jealous, etc. These feelings are what motivated historical and contemporary man to change our technological expression. Our judgement created expectations and the motivation to achieve many objectives that were expressed in technological terms.

Without judgement our mind would accept everything ensuring that nothing would change in our minds. Our minds are the source of our creative and emotional expression so without judgement we are at peace unable to contemplate changing a thing. The mind's judgement of *what is* is the exclusive cause of any psychological or emotional discontent. This discontent has led to many new discoveries that have alleviated suffering, disease and personal effort. The discontent caused by the mind's judgement has also led to much disparity, suffering and death.

Each observation that is made by the mind of each separate perspective is merely 'perception'. How we judge our experiences equates to our personal mind's perception of them. How we perceive our experiences is prejudiced by what we believe about those experiences. How we perceive our experience is the cause of any feeling that is not peace, joy or happiness. Our mind's judgement motivates us by preventing access to our peace, happiness and joy. We can only pursue peace, happiness and joy until we realise that only our mind's judgement can prevent it.

To realise peace we simply stop judging and start accepting what is. This is because what we emotionally respond to is our mind's individual perception. Our mind's perception is sustained by our judgement of what is. The critic is the judge. The critic is a separated part of us that is necessary for us to evolve our understanding of *what is* in order to transcend generic behavioural expression. Our motivation exists in the form of beliefs and hypotheses. Without judgement, there is only peace, joy, happiness and pain. Without duality we would not have evolved technology.

Without duality we could not have judged *what is* to be less than what it *should be.*

There is just one mind undivided. This means that without perceived separation there is nothing to judge or be judged. When there are two, there is the creator and his creation, the judge and the judged. Judgement with compassion is judgement that is wise. Judgement without compassion can be cruel, selfish, violent and greedy. There is only one mind separated by a multitude of separate perspectives. The price we pay for our judgement is our peace of mind.

A separate false mind is required within our true

Duality and Non-Duality

whole mind if we are to be free of the constraints of instinctual generic behavioural expression. We created a judgemental separate mind in order to transcend the generic expression of the animal kingdom. The fruit of this critical mind is technological evolution. The cost is our peace, joy and happiness. This is why we become addicted to the emotions that are exclusively created by judging *what is* to be good, bad, lazy, ugly, too fat, ignorant, unacceptable, terrifying, phobic, impossible, etc.

Our body's chemistry responds to how we perceive experience. Anyone that chooses non-duality has not realised that without it we would lose our ability to judge. One can't add to itself and one cannot take from itself. Each mind will eventually come to the realisation that all separate minds exist within one mind. Non-duality has never been disturbed by duality which is simply an illusion created by believing that we exist at a fixed location within the whole mind. This belief in an 'I' perspective created an 'identity' expressed as *I, me* and *mine.*

Perception is not vision, it is judgement projected. Duality and non-duality are merely concepts that only have a contextual existence beyond which their integrity is betrayed by the fact that in truth they do not exist. If we didn't create a perspective that could judge our legs to be too slow and too weak we would never have invented the cart, car, ship or train. The perceived duality was essential for technological evolution. We assume a critical perspective to judge the self and its environment in order to continue to evolve what is defined as technological expression.

A mind that is guided by compassion is truly

wise. Duality means 'I' perceives *my body* to be something unique to *me* that 'I' possess. The separation is merely sustained by installing an identity within the child's mind and populating it with beliefs. This conditioning replaces the child's vision and wisdom with beliefs. We are non-dual but our mind's awareness is separated by our belief in our identity. This perceived duality means that in truth we are 'non-dual'. Seeking non-duality is like me looking for myself. The self cannot find the self because the self is the self.

I can't find myself because 'I' am what 'I' am looking for. So if 'I' am what 'I' am looking for, why am I looking? We look to find the self because we know something is missing. What is missing is our awareness of the 'whole' of us because our awareness has become incarcerated within the perspective of a false self we call our identity. Non-duality is the truth. What we believe is just what we believe. The perception of duality is what creates the search for what we believe will lead to non-duality. Non-duality is the belief that we are less than 100% of our whole self.

We are whole but we have lost our awareness of our whole self because we believe we are *who* we believe we are. It is only if our mind can be domesticated that we can be persuaded to define our self and limit our awareness to that definition. Our awareness separates itself from the whole mind when we believe we are an identity. We were told we were our identity. We are what was named and identified according to others. You can call a dog by a name until it answers to that name and no other even though it is still what

Duality and Non-Duality

it was before its mind was domesticated.

Perceived enlightenment is temporarily experienced by the realisation and awareness of the unlimited whole mind that exists beyond the limits of the conditioned mind. There is no such thing as 'enlightenment'. If the conditioned mind's faith in its beliefs is gradually depleted the believer can gradually transcend and evolve the parameters of the false mind that sustains the borders of what is defined as 'duality'. Without duality the person who experiences the bliss that exists beyond the conditioned mind may appear psychotic, drunk, high or ungrounded.

The world as it is perceived is a reflection of a conditioned part of the *whole mind*. To transcend this separated part that is conditioned with beliefs is to lose touch with a reality that can only be perceived by a conditioned mind. The perceived duality is a miracle occurring within the whole mind that remains undisturbed by the hallucinations perceived by the conditioned mind. The *whole mind* is the source of unlimited ideas given in response to the judgement of a conditioned part within the whole mind. This separate part within the whole mind is called the ego mind.

Experience is God's Response to Faith

The life in each child is an expression of God. To ensure each innocent child does not realise its true identity it is persuaded to believe it is a *who* and not a *what*. In the moment an infant child begins to make its first effort at communication the parents will begin their attempts at installing an identity. The 'identity' is an existential operating system that is placed within the part of God's mind that sustains the child. Identities are installed to control behavioural expression. Each child loses awareness of its own source which is the mind of God when it places its faith in an identity.

The child severs the direct connection with its own source when it places its faith in the belief that it is an identity. Only faith permits the belief in an identity to enter the part of God's mind that is unique to that child. The *whole unlimited mind* is not personal. The collective mind is where all beliefs, knowledge and memories are stored. A computer's operating system allows separate software applications to be installed on the same hard drive. The operating system of the mind is language. The identity is an existential software application referred to as a *belief system*.

Faith permits archetypal belief systems to be installed into the *whole mind* through each child's ears. All a belief requires to enter and take up residence

EXPERIENCE IS GOD'S RESPONSE TO FAITH

within the mind is a believer's faith. Once believed, faith gives the beliefs the believer's power. Faith is the believer's power. The power of faith is limitless. Only a believer's faith has the authority to control the expression of a believer's *unlimited mind*. Only a believer's faith gives a belief the authority to take up residence within God's mind. The beliefs of family, religion and education are powerless without a believer's faith.

As the blind faith of religion will demonstrate, a belief without 'understanding' can still exert powerful influence or even take full control over a believer. Beliefs are the existential software that religion, media, education and marketing use to control or influence the mind's behavioural expression. A believer may never realise that it is *only their faith* in limitation that can limit the expression of their unlimited mind. The *one mind* that is the collective source of each individual body is autonomous. Each individual body does not have an autonomous separate mind.

We create what is perceived to be our separate autonomous mind by bearing false witness. Those who fell from grace are exiled from heaven. The whole mind of God is heaven. The only way that those who fell from grace could live on in the mind of God was by trespassing within the unique part of the mind given to each child. The devil uses the body of God's children for sin by installing existential software within the part of the mind that is unique to each child. The software is beliefs placed in the mind through the body's ears. The devil's greatest trick is to convince us that he is us.

The devil is the 'name' that uses our authority to

install an identity into the mind. Our faith is our authority. In the moment we place our faith in the belief that we are our given identity that 'devil' has our authority to take possession of the part of the mind that controls the body until the body dies or we withdraw our faith. The child's faith grants the devil admission into the whole mind to live a parasitic existence feeding on our energy. There is no personal separate mind. Each separate body has the same awareness but is experiencing the miracle of life from a unique bodily perspective.

Authority ensures the ears of each body are used to install beliefs within the unlimited mind. There is only one mind. What we call our personal mind is each body's *divine inheritance*. Once installed within the mind, the existential software that is the child's personal beliefs controls the mind's expression through that child. When educated, the unique expression of the unlimited mind through each child is controlled by what has the child's faith. A belief's control over the mind's expression is identical to the control that computer software has over a computer's functional expression.

Fear demonstrates there is no freedom in a mind controlled by beliefs. It is only our faith that makes us all believers. Every believer exists in a permanent trance that perceives a 'reality' sustained only by their faith. Soldiers, Muslims, Christians, Hindus, scientists, Americans and Europeans are examples of *archetypal mind programming*. Each individual's perception is prejudiced by the beliefs that define what they perceive to be reality. Perception limits what the mind sees by ensuring that nothing is perceived to exist beyond what is perceived to exist.

Experience is God's Response to Faith

The mind's perception is controlled by the official language of the 'dictionary'. An individual's ability to understand and communicate is equal to their vocabulary. The part of the mind that sustains each individual body is only limited by the faith each believer places in limiting beliefs. Incarcerating the mind with language ensures that language edits what the mind can see. Once installed, language is the exclusive medium that controls what we think, communicate and understand. There are two things that can trick a child into limiting the unlimited mind's ability to understand.

The first is the vocabulary installed using language. Our beliefs articulated with language act as gatekeepers that control what the believer can and cannot understand. Language ensures that any word that exceeds the vocabulary of an individual cannot be understood. The second thing that can limit a person's ability to understand is their faith in *conflicting beliefs*. Only our faith in beliefs can empower them. Beliefs are how to control what cannot be controlled. What cannot be controlled is an unlimited mind. Paradoxically, only the unlimited mind can control the unlimited mind.

An unlimited mind *can't* if a believer places its faith in *I can't*. An unlimited mind must learn if a believer believes he must learn. The mind places constraints upon its unlimited expression when a believer places their faith in limiting beliefs. To free our self we simply free our mind. We *free our mind* by withdrawing our faith in limiting beliefs. Placing our faith in beliefs that lack compassion is a 'sin'. Our faith in the belief that words were fact was used by others to install concepts. Only our faith in the concepts of 'enemy', 'infidel' and 'terrorist' could make them real for us.

If we withdrew our faith in those concepts they would be removed from our mind and they would no longer exist for us. The identity is an operating system founded on a set of prejudices which when believed define a 'self' that is unique and separate. The life that is expressed in every single body is a 'single' consciousness. There is only one consciousness that is expressed as the life in all things. The true self is everyone and everything we meet. We are each individually placing the one mind's faith in conflict reflected in family, friends, strangers and enemies.

Our life is a reflection of what has our faith. Our life is the effect of what has our faith. What has our faith is the cause and our life is the effect. Mankind is the self playing many different parts but refusing to realise and remember. MATTHEW 5:44, KJV *"But I say unto you, Love your enemies, bless them that curse you, do good to them that hate you, and pray for them that despitefully use you and persecute you"*. We are each separate expressions of the one consciousness that is the life in all things. You are me and I am you.

Consciousness is like water that fills every void and can adapt to any shape or condition. Rain can become a river and the river can become a drink and the drink can become us. In truth we are the life that is expressed in all things. A denial of others is a denial of self. Faith in a separate self is a denial of the whole self. Separate minds do not exist within the mind of God. Our bodies are separate but our collective mind is not. When we load separate software on to the same hard drive of a computer expressed as separate functions there is still only one hard drive.

There is only one mind sustaining many different perspectives. Our faith in the concept of separation created it within the mind. Our experience reflects what has our faith. Our perception of separate bodies created an experience of separate bodily perspectives each living separate lives. The separate perspectives of separate bodies with individual belief systems created what was perceived to be contrasting experiences. These separate testimonies led to a perceived understanding of what we came to call the 'world'.

In certain locations the world is different but this does not change the fact that there is only one world. To call Nigeria a different country to France does not change the fact there is only one world. The body is an invention of the mind to be used as an instrument for experience. The experience is the experience. Our 'existence' is the experience. Conflicting beliefs installed into the mind through separate bodies can create contrasting perceptions for the same experience. The operating systems that control the part of the mind that sustains the body of the parent controls the parents.

The parents use the eyes and ears of the body of their child to install language to programme the part of the mind that sustains that child. The operating system that controls the parents has a built in function called instinct to programme their own child's mind. The operating system is the 'identity'. Only the child's faith can permit an identity to enter the mind to sit on the child's throne in the kingdom. The child's mind is not in the brain. It is within the whole mind that is heaven. Placing faith in the identity permits *Satan* to sit upon the child's throne in the whole mind that is heaven.

Heaven is the kingdom of God. Heaven is the mind of God. The mind's software is a generic 'belief system' installed to control the expression of the part of the mind that is each individual child's divine inheritance. The mind of God sustains every separate body. The devil uses the child's faith in contrasting and conflicting beliefs to control the whole mind's expression through each body. Conflicting beliefs are the cause of all conflict on earth. The adaption of the body and the environment is the mind's response to the false witness of perception.

This adaption enables the body to transcend historical limitations. This perceived evolution can be detected over generations by reference to what is termed DNA. DNA is passed down from generation to generation as it continues to go through the process of 'evolution' and 'devolution'. What is defined as DNA is a collective belief system. The operating system is programmed by genetic code and updated by what has the believer's faith. This collective faith is passed down from generation to generation in the blood. The beliefs of each generation add to the collective DNA.

This is what is meant by the sins (beliefs) of the parents being visited upon their children. When consciousness is expressed through a body it does not know '*what it is*'. What we generically refer to as a dog does not need to know if it is a dog for it to exist. A dog is simply what we call what is represented by the word 'dog'. Factually what is represented by the word 'consciousness' is not consciousness. Consciousness is how our beliefs currently define the miracle that is life. Consciousness is the life that exists in everything. This life transcends all labels and definitions.

The qualities we use to define what we are experiencing are really just describing the limitations that our vocabulary places on our ability to see the miracle that is the life that exists in everything. As the generations and centuries passed the collective DNA has faithfully sustained a 'full record' of all those who came before. Our DNA is a sanctuary that allows our ancestors to live on in us. The *conscious evolution* of the mind through the mortal perspective requires an instrument that we call the body. Our faith in beliefs creates a benchmark that is proven or disproven by experience.

The experience was the truth that evolved the mind by transcending the limitations of historical beliefs. Our personal limitations can only exist for the period that our beliefs have our faith. Placing our faith in an identity is self-deception. The true self is an unlimited mind that has no judgement or objection because it has no limitations. It was only by placing our faith in limitations and problems that we were able to evolve in technological terms. If we did not judge *what is* to be less than what it should be we would not have evolved beyond simple technologies.

To retain the technologies we developed beliefs and hypothesis that were passed down from parent to child. We did this without wisdom not realising that whilst the belief in words retained knowledge, that faith would create limitations within our unlimited minds. Identities were once what the body did. Some were blacksmiths, merchants, farmers, carpenters, tailors, fishermen and soldiers. Some were identified by the class or caste into which they were born. Religion created generic identities and rules to be obeyed by the 'faithful'.

Religions justified their position by reference to an authority given to them alone by God. The expression of God in each new born child was rejected and replaced by a religious identity that programmed the mind. This was an attempt to use the child's faith to limit the expression of God on earth. Free will means God does not challenge any belief that has our faith. Our beliefs are not our truth they are our jailors. EXODUS 20:16, KJV "*thou shalt not bear false witness against thy neighbour*". Slavery of the mind is slavery of the body. If you control the mind you control the body.

Faith Creates Poverty or Wealth

Crime is a destructive shortcut out of poverty. A life of crime is a life of chance. When the person commits the crime he becomes his behaviour and puts his body's freedom of expression at risk. Life doesn't show us where the karmic traps lay. To discover the wealth that is without we must discover the wealth that is within. To discover love in the world we must discover the love within us. To conquer the world and its temptations the seeker must *realise* he is what he seeks. If we discover the self we discover the richest treasure which is the source of life itself.

When we discover the self we realise that being born into a family of wealth or one living in poverty cannot diminish our faith's power to create poverty or wealth. It is within his own mind that a man's fortunes are won and lost. Within our mind we may be the most desperate among men or the happiest, richest and most successful. We obtain, lose and regain health and riches according to what we put our mind's faith in. To experience one of these contrasting experiences is to live without balance. A life without balance is the result of a mind that lacks the wisdom of compassion.

Poverty results from a mind that deprives the 'self' in order to conform and worship a self that lacks. Within our mind we can create a world of peace, joy, happiness and 'abundance but many choose to worship beliefs that deny and reject those possibilities. The mind's faith in beliefs that define the self as incapable, lacking or undeserving are prayers that are always answered. The power of our faith in *I cannot* is a prayer our 'unlimited mind' must deliver in the form of a life of limitation and struggle. Our wealth or poverty is the reward of our mind's faith.

We each create the world our mind perceives. To wish for a better world is to refuse to accept the world we created. To become a musician we must learn to play the instrument. PROVERBS 10:4, KJV, "*He becometh poor that dealeth with a slack hand: but the hand of the diligent maketh rich.*" The mind is an instrument that can do anything when we withdraw our mind's faith in all beliefs that exist in the context of *I cannot.* The second coming refers to the removal of the veil (perception) sustained by beliefs within the mind. The mind's faith gives the beliefs the believer's power.

The 'second coming' enables the incarcerated mind of the innocent child that was usurped by its own beliefs to awaken so that it can be *born again.* MATTHEW 18:3, KJV: *"And said, Verily I say unto you, Except ye be converted, and become as little children, ye shall not enter into the kingdom of heaven."* With our faith our mind creates our experience. We are the creator of our experience. MARK 8:36, KJV: "*For what shall it profit a man, if he shall gain the whole world, and lose his own soul?*" We are the soul. Our power is our faith. God's power is expressed through our faith.

What is God? God is the *greater understanding* that exists beyond all beliefs that were created to define what we perceive to be reality. That reality is only sustained for as long as our collective mind's faith holds the beliefs that sustain our perceived reality to be true. The hypothesis is the limit of our perception according to our vocabulary's observation. Our observation is prejudiced by what we believe. What we believe is that each word is what it represents. We have incarcerated our unlimited mind within the jurisdiction of our vocabulary.

We existed before language. We have programmed our minds with language and our wisdom has been replaced by what we believe. We can only believe what we do not know. Each belief that has our minds faith is given control over our mind. The mind controls the body's voluntary personal expression. Each belief's power is as strong as our faith. Our faith in each belief about the self sows a seed in the mind that must come to fruition when germinated by experience. Our ideas are our creative potential. Our faith is a catalyst for converting dreams and nightmares into experience

We must have faith before our mind can bring our self into existence. What is the 'self'? The self is our unlimited creative expression. The only thing that can prevent our unlimited creative expression is our faith in any belief that exists in the context of *I cannot*. If I believe I cannot become successful, I have given my mind's allegiance to the seed of this prayer and my fertile mind must deliver thoughts and feelings that ensure I never become successful. If I withdraw my faith in this seed my mind is open to other possibilities. The possibilities are endless.

We never left heaven. We have the power but not the wisdom to define the self. Our faith created a limited self that became the victim of its own judgement within the kingdom. MATTHEW 13:31, KJV: *"The kingdom of heaven is like to a grain of mustard seed, which a man took, and sowed in his field."* We lost awareness of the kingdom of heaven when we placed a veil upon our eyes existing as our perception. When we judged *what is*, we replaced it with what we judged it to be. Judgement in the form of an evolving educated perspective took the place of our own inherent wisdom.

ISAIAH 44:9: *"They that make a graven image are all of them vanity; and their delectable things shall not profit; and they are their own witnesses; they see not, nor know; that they may be ashamed."* When we believe I cannot the power of our mind's faith means that we cannot transcend this belief. MATHEW 17:20 *"And Jesus said unto them, Because of your unbelief: for verily I say unto you, If ye have faith as a grain of mustard seed, ye shall say unto this mountain, Remove hence to yonder place; and it shall remove; and nothing shall be impossible unto you."*

Beliefs are prayers that are always answered. Why believe in limitation if this sows a seed that always comes to fruition. We did not forbid our self any fruit including poverty, slavery, starvation, sexual violence, war and incarceration. These are the fruits of prayers that are always answered by our omnipotent mind. *I cannot* is the mantra of a victim, victimised by his own faith in beliefs that 'trespass against him'. Unbelief is a lack of faith. Unbelief is the removal of our faith in our beliefs. We do not need to become an unbeliever but we do need to withdraw our faith in *I cannot*.

I cannot is how an omnipotent mind can limit its

Faith Creates Poverty or Wealth

creative expression by 'checkmating' itself with its own power. The devil requires the believer to believe *I cannot* to ensure the believer's omnipotent mind uses its own faith to incarcerate itself within the jurisdiction of its beliefs. 'Un-belief' is a lack of any beliefs existing in the context of *I cannot*. Love cannot be where fear is, so until we withdraw our faith in fearful beliefs our mind cannot replace fearful constraints with the alternative. Poverty or wealth is the answer to our prayers and a testament to the power of faith.

Faith is God's Power

Many religions imply or openly behave as if they have God's authority. Religion holds God to be perfect, omnipotent, omnipresent and existing as the life in all things. The mind's creative expression cannot exceed what has the mind's faith. The mind's faith in its beliefs gives those beliefs the power of the mind. What we think and talk about reveals our mind's awareness. Those who wish for a better life have not realised that their beliefs are designing a life their mind is creating. Our faith in our beliefs gives them the power to control our mind. Beliefs have no power without faith.

If we believe the world is 'evil', 'cruel', 'mad' and 'chaotic' it causes our mind to generate those types of *psychologically induced emotional responses.* The mind's vocabulary reveals which beliefs control our mind. Each belief programmes the brain to release specific chemicals in response to the mind's perception. If we define our self using the terms 'frustration', 'anger', 'upset', 'helpless' and 'embarrassment' our brain releases chemical feelings to match those terms. Our faith in the beliefs that define perception gives those beliefs control over the mind's perception.

Perception is the main cause of any loss of peace of mind. Our perception causes the brain to release chemicals that control voluntary self-expression. When we allow beliefs to programme our mind's perception

Faith is God's Power

our perception creates our experience. If our mind uses its power to see a world that is peaceful, fun and joyful it will cause the brain to release matching chemical responses. What does this mean? It means that happiness is a choice. *All psychologically induced emotional responses* are caused by a form of 'spiritual alchemy' that is powered by the mind's faith.

We are educated to believe in politics, economics, theology, religion, industry, tax, profit, loans, debt, conflict, war, disease and justification. Our mind's faith brings these concepts into existence *within our mind*. What man worships above all things is not God it is *money*. Faith in money uses 'spiritual alchemy' to make it more valuable 'in the mind' than what it can buy. The most valuable thing in existence is the faith of each new born child. Whoever has the child's faith has God's power. Nothing can exist within the mind without faith.

Concepts cannot enter or exist within the mind without the believer's faith. The sacred paradox is that the believer's faith in beliefs gives those beliefs the power to 'usurp' the believer by taking control of his mind. Our relationship with God is beyond the limitations of any religious beliefs that prohibit the full creative expression of the whole mind. The mind is an instrument through which we express our inheritance. Our inheritance is our *unlimited creative expression*. Only limiting beliefs that have the minds faith can incarcerate the mind's unlimited creative expression.

If a mind believes that $2 + 2 = 5$, this belief contextually determines the limits of the mind's understanding. If the same mind withdraws its faith in this belief the limitation is removed. A correct or incorrect answer does not reveal intelligence, it reveals 'understanding'. Understanding is determined by what we believe or know about what we are experiencing. The mind of a believer can always change what it believes or knows. Freedom from suffering is achieved by the withdrawal of the mind's faith in beliefs that lack compassion. Compassion is the feelings of others.

Foundations of Clay

Every book that contains the word of God is not the word of God. The message is constrained by the words and language of the messenger. The personal vocabulary of the individual who receives a message from God is the 'medium' through which God speaks. This means that whilst each book may contain the word of God it is not the word of God. This is because the ability of the messenger is limited by their personal vocabulary and God is not limited. Any word that exceeds the limits of the personal vocabulary of the mind of the one who hears it cannot be understood by that mind.

The ability to articulate a message is determined by the messenger's vocabulary. The vocabulary of the recipient of the message establishes the limits of their understanding of words. 'Stories', 'parables', 'allegories' and 'metaphors' are used to convey messages through understanding beyond the limits of the mind's vocabulary. If the written word is not understood a reader may seek the opinion of others who will act as an interpreter or authority for particular books. Many argue that the bible is the word of God, valuable, accurate, inaccurate or a series of parables or metaphors.

There are many religions, theologians, academic experts and holy men who by comparison interpret the scriptures to have different and sometimes conflicting meanings. It is not possible for the mind to realise greater understanding if it has given its allegiance to a particular belief about anything. This is because a belief filters and prejudices the perception of the believer's mind. Our faith in a belief excludes and rejects other possibilities that are in conflict with that belief. A believer cannot know truth because what is known requires no faith in belief or hypothesis.

Our beliefs are the foundation of our faith. Only our faith in our beliefs can prevent greater understanding. When we put our faith in false gods, like money, fame, selfishness or a reward in heaven for engaging in religious war we are selfishly looking to acquire something. Truth is a solid foundation. We forget or deny our truth when we believe we must become something. Regardless of any perceived imperfection, each one of us is born perfect, as were our parents before us. The truth of our existence is built upon foundations that are solid.

MATTHEW 7:24-27, KJV, *"Therefore whosoever heareth these sayings of mine, and doeth them, I will liken him unto a wise man, which built his house upon a rock: And the rain descended, and the floods came, and the winds blew, and beat upon that house; and it fell not: for it was founded upon a rock. And every one that heareth these sayings of mine, and doeth them not, shall be likened unto a foolish man, which built his house upon the sand: And the rain descended, and the floods came, and the winds blew, and beat upon that house; and it fell: and great was the fall of it."*

Our foundation does not require beliefs to make the miracle of our existence real and cannot be replaced with what is unreal hiding behind beliefs that exist in the form of hypothesis. The naming of a child replaces the solid foundations of the true identity with a false self that does not rest upon the solid foundations of truth, but upon the beliefs of those who sought to define the child, its reality and the child's place in it. When we believe we are who we are told we are, our house is built upon foundations of beliefs. It is because truth can replace beliefs that these are foundations of clay.

Before any mind is limited by a single belief its potential is unlimited. The mind is a rock that is unlimited and unaffected by 'truth'. We require no beliefs. When we know we have no need of beliefs. We do not need beliefs to learn to walk, talk and express ourselves. The name used by our parents to define us hypnotises our mind in the moment that we believe we are 'it'. The 'identity' is clay because it requires a believer for its existence, but the believer is the rock of truth. We are therefore real but our beliefs are not. We are the truth that cannot be washed away or eroded.

Every word in the dictionary is a 'belief'. We believe each word is what it represents. We have defined everything observed in existence with beliefs to control our mind's ability to perceive and communicate. All perception is limited by a vocabulary that is based upon a belief in words. The simplicity or complexity of any hypothesis is determined by the vocabulary of the person in whose mind it is created. When we believe something that is written which is not our personal experience we deprive our self of the mystery and experience that is our 'personal truth'.

Each belief usurps direct experience sometimes preventing the personal discovery of our unique truth in those experiences. The greatest discoveries come from those whose perception is not constrained by generic definitions or superstitious beliefs. To believe is to deprive oneself of the divine mystery of the adventure of life and to prejudge it according to our mind's personal prejudices. This is what prevents our enjoyment and is the cause of what is defined as 'boredom'. There is nothing missing which means there is no hole to fill.

There is no hole to fill because we are created whole. 'What do you want to be when you grow up?' is a question that encourages us to judge and reject the self in order to create an archetype that we spend our formative years working to become. Becoming someone else is a rejection of the self. The gods of democratic freedom, money, war, politics and fear, require our collective faith in them to have any power over our mind. Without those false gods in our life, we will still exist but they will not! They are built on foundations of clay. The clay is our mind's faith existing as 'belief'.

Heaven

Heaven is our whole mind. Hell is an illusion that our faith allows to exist within our whole mind. Hell is a belief system that was created to incarcerate us. It is our own faith that incarcerates us in hell. Heaven or hell is a choice that our faith decides. Only faith can empower a belief. Beliefs sustain all psychological limitations. Our faith in limiting beliefs denies us our own freedom. The cause of all psychological fear is *faith*. It is the faith placed in fearful beliefs that causes fearful feelings. Our creative expression is limited by our beliefs. It is not our ability that determines the limits of our personal expression it is what we believe.

All personal expression is controlled by the specific beliefs that have our faith. Without exception what has our faith has our power. Faith gave our belief system exclusive control of our personal expression. To control or limit a child's expression you must first obtain their faith in a number of limiting beliefs. Unless a child's mind is free its behaviour will reflect what it believes. Religions require 'followers' to place their faith in beliefs created to ensure behavioural expression conforms to a *religious archetype.* An archetypal identity is a 'behavioural model' that prescribes the parameters of voluntary behavioural expression.

'Hell' is a conditioned mind that is created when a believer's faith is placed in limiting beliefs. Generic beliefs are designed to programme our perception of everything *including our self.* A believer's mind is conditioned by their family, religion, peers and education. When each word in the dictionary is believed to be fact, each word's *definition* replaces what it was created to define within a believer's mind. Once a word's definition is understood it controls what we think and feel when exposed to what the word defines. Psychological 'fear' of any stimulus is what causes the brain to release fearful neurochemical responses to that stimulus.

How we define an experience will determine what we feel in that experience. The conditioning of a child's mind is the main objective of education. A well behaved child is a child that has adapted well to the *archetypal conditioning* of their religion and community. A phobia demonstrates that our perception can programme our mind to trigger neurological responses to any stimulus that we fear. We must believe that each word in the dictionary is what it represents before each word's definition becomes our personal truth. The objective of education is to ensure that perceived reality does not exceed the official definition.

It takes just one individual to define the world in new terms for man's perception of the whole world to transform. Change results from transcending the limits of generic perception. Jesus, Mohammad, Buddha, Ghandi, Einstein and Jung enabled many to transcend dogmatic limitations sustained by their faith. Dogma uses faith to deny the realisation of greater understanding. When we limit our understanding of everything in existence to the official word's definition we deny any greater understanding. If I need to employ you to clean and cook for me I must ensure that you do not lose your reliance upon me to sustain you.

A conditioned mind keeps a slave a slave and a soldier a soldier. The census and christening is not done for any other reason than to ensure an existential operating system is placed within every child's mind before its awareness can 'realise'. The operating system of the mind is an 'identity'. To programme a child's mind the parent calls out to their child's using a name until they receive a response. Only by obtaining a child's faith can beliefs remain within their mind. Only the beliefs that have our faith can gain admittance into our mind. If a child believes it is limited, its faith in this belief is powerful enough to create a life of limitation.

The greatest trick of the devil is to disguise himself as our 'name'. The child's faith in the 'given name' admits the devil into the child's mind to take the child's place. We cannot be the name if we are what is named. Each and every single belief is a 'prayer' to God that is always answered. The devil uses the voices of our parents to convince us to place our faith in the belief that we are the 'name' we hear them call Demonic beliefs always lack compassion. We each believe our identity is 'me'. The beliefs that have our faith have total control over our mind and body. The only power that incarcerates' a child of God in *hell* is its own faith.

If we try to escape the existential constraints created and sustained by the faith we place in our beliefs we will feel the neurochemical response called 'fear'. Our beliefs 'pre-programme' neurochemical responses. For example, if we need the salary from our job to pay the rent and also believe that sickness may cause us to lose our job, sickness may create the neurochemical response called 'stress'. The underlying cause of perceptually induced neurochemical responses is always faith. If we withdraw our faith in the beliefs that sustain our perception it is impossible to experience *perceptually induced neurochemical responses.*

Happiness cannot be found because happiness is not lost. Our neurochemical responses mask our happiness. Our happiness is a permanent state that can only be trespassed against by the faith we place in the beliefs that judge our self, others and the world. MATTHEW 7:1-3 KJV *"Judge not, that ye be not judged. For with what judgment ye judge, ye shall be judged: and with what measure ye mete, it shall be measured to you again/ And why beholdest thou the mote that is in thy brother's eye, but considerest not the beam that is in thine own eye?"* Happiness is 'self-acceptance'. Happiness is the expression of the Love of God.

How we perceive our self, others and our experiences will determine how we respond in neurochemical terms. A conditioned mind is the most effective method for creating fixed neurochemical responses to pre-defined stimulus. How we perceive our self determines how we generally feel in emotional terms. It is by programming the perception of the masses through religion, education and propaganda that you control what they feel when exposed to any stimulus that has been pre-defined by those organisations. An individual's perception may cause them to deny any desires that are in conflict with personal or religious obligations.

Fulfilled desires that are in breach of a religious or cultural obligation may create guilt, leading to depression or addiction and condemnation of the self. Guilt is a complex that creates neurochemical responses. When our judgement of our self and the world floods our system with neurochemicals that do not feel good we may say that we do not *feel* happy. This is a misunderstanding. Depression is describing a 'soup' of neurochemical responses caused by our own judgement. Our salvation cannot be found in the perceived world or in pharmaceutical products. Our salvation can only come from withdrawing our faith in beliefs.

What is defined as depression is simply a complex of the mind sustained by a metaphorical software programme called the *belief system*. It is the beliefs that have our faith that cause the neurochemical responses that are diagnosed as depression. The cause of our depression is our own faith. The existence of beliefs that cause psychological maladies is sustained exclusively by the faith we place in them. If we withdraw our faith in our beliefs they become nothing more than a hypothesis. When we withdraw our faith in all beliefs that lack compassion peace is restored to our mind and we are no longer a threat to our self or others.

Once we believe that each word is what it was created to represent we create an internal representation within our mind called 'knowledge'. It is difficult to fight the neurochemical responses that disturb our peace of mind. This is why so many people meditate. If successful our meditation provides us with brief moments of escape from the noise and thoughts within our mind caused by our unique personal complex. Our personal psychological complex is our *belief system.* The personal belief system of each person is unique. We are the believer. Our unlimited mind's expression cannot exceed the limitations of any belief that has our faith.

The potential of every mind is 'unlimited'. The power that fuels our mind's expression is our faith. With faith nothing is impossible. Therefore the only limits that can be placed upon our creative expression are those that are sustained by the faith we place in *personal limitations.* With faith, *I can't* is as powerful in its effect as *I can* but neither of these prayers define what *I am*. The measurable achievements of separate individuals with contrasting beliefs can be significant. Each life is a testimony to the beliefs that have a believer's faith. Life is a conversion of our faith into our experience. Our life is the product of what has our faith.

Perception requires a vocabulary. Our vocabulary is equal to the number of words that we learn, understand, remember and use to create and sustain our beliefs. Those with the greatest vocabulary have the greatest potential to realise freedom of expression. Those who create new terms to replace older terms are creating opportunities for the whole world to transcend generic behavioural expression. Some of the terms that have transformed historical expression are 'religion', 'enlightenment', 'computers', software', 'music', 'medicine', 'internet', 'entertainment', 'holidays', 'psychology', 'media', 'technology', 'politics', 'science', 'physics' and 'sport'.

Many forms of expression that we now take for

granted were once prevented by authorities who vicariously controlled our minds by obtaining our faith in *their beliefs*. In history when free minds shared their experiences they were accused of heresy for which the punishment was death. Any religion that requires us to place our faith in a false self is evil. It is devil worshippers who violently enforce laws to prevent compassionate freedom of expression. Our perceived body only exists within our mind. This means that our perception of our body in literal terms can evolve and devolve it. Our body is a work in progress of our own making.

The world that we perceive is a projection of our mind's programming. The seen world reflects a projection of our understanding that we call 'perception'. We are consciousness. We are the life that is manifested in our own body. We are not the instrument that is the body we inhabit. In the moment we accept the testimony of our maternal parents as true our faith gives their words our power to control our mind. Our power is our faith. When we believe that we are our body we become limited by the perceived limitations of that body. When we believe we are the words that others use to define us we are hypnotised by our own faith.

The 'autonomic system' is the genetic legacy of our ancestors. Our beliefs will evolve or devolve the autonomic system of our offspring. DNA is a biological operating system that evolves with each generation. The ego usurps the body's inherent awareness by obtaining our faith in its beliefs. The ego is the 'devil'. Frankenstein is a metaphor for the false self that our faith created. We are the God that creates the ego *in our own image.* Faith in an identity traps our awareness within a false mind that must be programmed to function. 'Words' are metaphorical code and beliefs are the metaphorical software of a *false mind.*

The existential software that controls our mind is created by assembling language into a series of instructions that are commonly referred to as 'beliefs'. *Belief systems* sustain religions, caste systems, aristocracy, royalty, political ideologies, economic systems, psychological complexes, personal prejudices, patriotism, racism, misogyny, misandry, hatred and institutional biases.

There are reported to be approximately 196 countries in the world. So what sort of global psychological complex will be created in the collective mind of man if we all place our faith in the belief that we must be 'patriotic'?

We are Christ. Our false ego self is the 'anti-Christ'. The ego is no longer referred to as the devil, *but it is.*
How we define this false self creates a context for our existence. What we believe about our self establishes the parameters we have placed upon our freedom of expression. It was our own parents who replaced us with an identity of their choosing. LUKE 12:53 KJV *"The father shall be divided against the son, and the son against the father; the mother against the daughter, and the daughter against the mother; the mother in law against her daughter in law, and the daughter in law against her mother in law."*

When we believe we are who we are told we are we exist in an existential paradox as both the believer and the belief. In terms of destiny what we believe about our self we become. At some point we realise that the identity that used our faith to take our place is not who or what we are. The false self is not us, it is just a caricature that we believe is us. The paradox is the creator and the creation existing as one. The 'saviour' believes he needs saving only because he believes he is who he believes he is. We are each the creator of the creation that we mistakenly believe is our whole self. We were given an identity so we cannot be it.

The way to our salvation is to transcend the limited perspective of our identity. The identity is a *false self* that resides within our mind. This false self obtained our faith in order to control us. We created the ego in our own image. It now controls us with a belief system. Unhappiness is caused by placing our faith in beliefs. No belief can remain within our mind without our faith. Our beliefs control our perceptually induced neurochemical responses. If we remove our faith in the beliefs that sustain perception peace will be restored to our mind and body. Many look back on their childhood feeling resentment towards their own parents.

It we do not have experiences that 'feel emotionally painful' we could not learn or grow to eventually realise greater understanding. Whilst most are not consciously aware of it, it is because it was our own parents who placed us within the parameters of a false identity that many of us feel anger and resentment towards our parents. Our parents are innocent because as children they were also tricked into allowing demonic trespassers to enter and take control of their mind. Those demonic trespassers are beliefs. Our faith is the only thing powerful enough to constrain us. For a belief to exert power over us it must first obtain our faith.

Our parents used our love for them to obtain our faith in a false self. Without our faith this false self could not enter the Garden of Eden. The Christ in us died for our sins but is resurrected through repentance. Sin is belief. Forgiveness is repentance. Forgiveness is the withdrawal of our faith in all beliefs that lack compassion. MATTHEW 6:14-15 "*For if ye forgive men their trespasses, your heavenly Father will also forgive you: But if ye forgive not men their trespasses, neither will your Father forgive your trespasses.*" Forgiveness leads to the death of our false self and the resurrection of our Christ self so that we can be born again.

Unless we become divided against the identity given to us by our own family it will consume us. Whilst we believe we are our identity we are not fully alive or dead. The artistic expression of Frankenstein, vampires and zombies reveals an unconscious awareness of man's condition. Artistic expression reveals an unconscious awareness of our existential predicament. The devil is our own creation, created with the power of our own faith in the moment that we believe we are who we are told we are. Most have not yet realised that our given identity is an *archetypal image* created within the mind of someone else.

Every war shows us that whilst we believe we are our given identity we will destroy anything that threatens the survival of that existence. The ego is the devil. We will fight for our ignorance. We will fight for our cruelty. We will fight for our possessions. We will fight to deny facts. Surrendering to God is the 'death' of the false self. It is God fearing because when we surrender to God this false self will die in order that the child our faith denies can be born again so that we may live. JOHN 3:3 KJV *"Jesus answered and said unto him, Verily, verily, I say unto thee, Except a man be born again, he cannot see the kingdom of God."*

We exist in a state of self-hypnosis. We have become obsessed with this false self that we each believe is me. We remain obsessed with this false self until the day we die or the day we realise. Selfishness is how we describe this self-obsession. The whole world is merely an image that reflects the perception of this false self who we each believe is our whole self. To expect love from the world is to misunderstand the world. Love is within. Love is not without. Love can only be expressed. This means that love cannot be found, it can only be realised. There is only one of us, divided by as infinite number of perspectives.

Each body is a separate perspective of the one consciousness that exists in all life. We are the one life that exists in all things. Heaven is the whole mind of the believer. Hell is a false mind containing our judgemental beliefs. Heaven is realised by withdrawing our faith in all the beliefs that create the neurological responses that the dictionary defines as 'emotional responses'. An empty mind is a peaceful mind. An empty mind is not an ignorant mind. By withdrawing our faith in our beliefs we undo the effect that each word's 'spell' has placed on our awareness and transcend the limitations of our belief system. Heaven is our whole mind.

Hell

There is darkness in the mind. This is a personal hell in which demons exist. This is an underworld that exists within our mind. Hell is sustained by our faith in beliefs that replace the world with our perception of it. Each individual mind's perception is personal. Language perceives what we call 'Earth' and what we generically define to be 'reality'. The words that have our mind's faith determine if we live in heaven or hell. Some concepts enforce the will of demons. Demons are concepts that can only exist in our mind as personal beliefs for as long as they have our minds faith.

Each demonic concept is a word that replaces what is real by defining reality. From the moment a mind is hypnotised to believe that each word is what it represents that mind's perception is defined, incarcerated and controlled by those words. Our mind is free to assemble words to construct our personal beliefs. Our beliefs determine the quality of our life. Every mind is controlled by its beliefs. Perception is the projection of beliefs. Perception is a false witness creating a personal world. In this world what passes for love are thoughts and feelings generated by perception.

Hell is not a metaphor. Hell is created within the mind in the moment we place our mind's faith in the particular words that create a specific version of reality. Robbery, violence, hatred, rape and murder create

Hell

hell. Those acts are justified and sustained by language. Language is the operating system of the mind. The mind controls the body of those who commit violent acts. Language has absolute control over any mind that thinks, understands and communicates with words. Each word is not what it represents. Any concept that justifies denying our compassion is demonic.

Words such as 'justification', 'courage' and patriotism' were created to programme the mind. If our mind worships those concepts we can justify denying our compassion. Our faith in demonic concepts grants them admission into our mind. The identity is the original sinner who has travelled down through each generation. We must realise that if we are the believer we are not our beliefs. If we do not realise we will place these concepts into the minds of our children and our children's children. With our faith each belief has the power to control our thoughts and feelings.

The only way to transcend the mind's judgemental convictions is through forgiveness. We are the trespasser that has travelled through all generations in the words used to condition each child's innocent mind. Once believed each word programmes the mind to control what the mind thinks and the body feels. Freedom of mind and body can only come through the mind's awakening. We must realise our mistake so that we can forgive our self. All judgement is a belief trespassing within our mind. Those trespassers are reflected in everything that is perceived by the mind.

We forgive those who trespass against us because they are innocent. All minds have been programmed with beliefs. Hell was created by man in the moment he judged *what is* to be less than what it should be.

When we judge each other we put the self above others creating hell on earth. We deny this by concealing it within concepts. Our mind creates our experience sustained by the veil of perception. Perception is the projection of beliefs which replace *truth* with personal prejudices. This phenomenon is also represented by the word 'hypnosis'. Heaven is peace of mind.

I can or I cannot is a Choice

To accept what we cannot change in this moment is to accept our self and our situation. If we do not accept our self or our situation, our mind creates thoughts of discontentment and feelings that we may describe as hopelessness, boredom, frustration or anger. In the moment we create a belief that we are hopeless, bored or frustrated with our situation our thoughts and feelings must serve this judgement. If our situation feels hopeless it is because we believe that it is. Our beliefs are the cause and what we think and our emotional responses are the effects.

Our faith is our power. If we give our faith to our beliefs our beliefs have our power. Putting our mind's faith in a belief is like placing software in the most powerful and unlimited computer in the universe. If we load software into our mind at five years of age and do not change it, the limits of its benefit and contextual integrity will eventually become apparent. It is inevitable that each and every belief about the self will become a limitation. All beliefs are limitations within a mind that is limitless. The beliefs we hold about reality determine our mind's relationship with reality.

The mind is contextually incarcerated by any belief the mind holds about the self for the period of time that the belief has our mind's faith. If we are unemployed and judge unemployment to be awful, we can feel awful because we indirectly perceive our self as being awful. If we judge our experience to be boring we will feel bored. If we judge something to be difficult we experience difficulty. The difficulty is caused by our belief that what we find difficult 'is difficult'. Paradoxically our mind is so powerful that it cannot exceed its own judgement.

To believe *I can't* ensures that our mind checkmates itself by disconnecting the believer from their own creative source. *I can't* is a command by the mind to the mind. 'I 'can-not' establishes the limits of *I can*. The source of the mind is unlimited. *I can't* is proof of the mind's omnipotence. *I can't* is proof that we even have the power to overpower and inhibit our unlimited creative expression. *I can't* is like a 'what if' feature in a spreadsheet. *I can't* is a command that establishes the limits of *I can*. Our faith in *I can't* is a denial and rejection by the mind of *I can*.

Any belief we put our mind's faith in installs spiritual software that controls the mind. Our faith in our beliefs is what gives them control over us. HEBREWS 11.1, KJV, *"Now faith is the substance of things hoped for, the evidence of things not seen."* So when we put our faith in the belief *I can't* our 'prayer' is always answered. All beliefs about our self are prayers and our prayers are always answered. The truth of us is that we can! To transcend the limitations in our life we must withdraw our faith in any beliefs that define us and our experience in limited terms.

The cause of addiction is the low feelings our mind's judgement creates. All emotions are the effect of our judgment. When we judge an experience to be boring, fun or fearful, we issue a command to our mind that our body's chemistry must obey in psychological and emotional terms. All emotions are chemical responses to how our beliefs define and therefore judge our experience. Matthew 7:1-2, KJV, *"Judge not, that ye be not judged. For with what judgment ye judge, ye shall be judged: and with what measure ye mete, it shall be measured to you again."*

We must remove *I can't* from our vocabulary unless it prevents us from doing evil. The power to believe *I can't* was granted in order to make our compassion absolute. I can't kill, I can't rape and I can't cause suffering are commands that ensure the mind cannot cause suffering. Without our faith in the belief *I cannot* we can. Out of compassion we were each given the freedom and power to install powerful constraints within our own mind. It is by compassionately applying the command *I can't* within the mind that we ensure that our mind *cannot* break the Ten Commandments.

Installing the command *I can't* without wisdom is how we created fears and phobias. We have the power to be compassionate, selfish or even powerless. Applied without wisdom the belief *I cannot* will create a life of suffering and limitation. Applied with wisdom our mind has the power to create a wonderful life. A wise mind is a mind that is guided by compassion. Compassion is denied by those who are evil because compassion means the attacker feels what the victim feels when they insult them, bully them, attack them, rape them or kill them.

When we are compassionate we feel what others feel. So if we victimise others we are victimised by their feelings. An eye for an eye! With compassion, if our victim feels fear, we merge with this feeling and it is us who feels fear in 'chemical' terms. Luke 6:31 *"And as ye would that men should do to you, do ye also to them likewise."* *I can* is the truth. It is only because I can believe that *I can-not* that I cannot. We are the believer not the belief. Beliefs require faith for their existence. Salvation is freedom. We free our mind by withdrawing our mind's faith in our beliefs. *I can* is our truth!

Idolatry

The ego is a false self created within our mind to control our mind. We create the ego to become the person that others will accept. To conform to the expectations of others is to deny our own true self. We each reject what God created by disguising, denying or embellishing natural thoughts and behaviour to ensure we conform to or exceed the expectations of others. Once our perceived self is believed to be 'me' it takes total possession of our mind. When we believe *it* is me we will deny truth rather than cause embarrassment to this *ego identity* that possesses our mind's faith.

What controls our thoughts and feelings are the beliefs that control our mind. We must consistently be *who* and *what* we say we are in order to ensure that people perceive the part we play. Once we create the identity that we wish to project, how other people perceive us becomes more important than how we feel. To deny our feelings is a denial of the 'true self' which is a denial of God. To avoid judgement the mind creates an idol that we aspire to become. If we do not realise that the ego is *not us* we may not realise that our mind's faith gives it control over our whole mind.

The mind can reject the sight of its own body if its perception is programmed with concepts that judge its own body. Self-denial can only exist if there is an idol or standard with which to compare. Idolatry is the mind's worship of an idol that looks and behaves in conformance with the 'graven image' created for the perception of others. The whole world is worshipping the graven images of celebrities, politicians and corporations. Those who actively support brands, institutions and corporations are 'idolaters' whose minds are worshipping the concepts those idols promote.

1 Corinthians 6:9-11, KJV, *"Know ye not that the unrighteous shall not inherit the kingdom of God? Be not deceived: neither fornicators, nor idolaters, nor adulterers, nor effeminate, nor abusers of themselves with mankind, Nor thieves, nor covetous, nor drunkards, nor revilers, nor extortioners, shall inherit the kingdom of God. And such were some of you: but ye are washed, but ye are sanctified, but ye are justified in the name of the Lord Jesus, and by the Spirit of our God."* If the architects of our mind's evolution are 'concepts' created for selfish gain then we worship the self.

The concepts of 'style', 'cool', 'respectable', 'exclusive', 'individual' are examples of vainglory. Philippians 2:3, KJV, *"Let nothing be done through strife or vainglory; but in lowliness of mind let each esteem other better than themselves."* A mind educated with concepts is limited by those concepts. To judge the self by comparing it with external concepts, archetypes or exemplars is 'judgement'. Matthew, 7:1-2, KJV, *"Judge not, that ye be not judged. For with what judgment ye judge, ye shall be judged: and with what measure ye mete, it shall be measured to you again."*

We are born perfect. A disabled person is born perfect. A poor person is born perfect. We are each a

IDOLATRY

perfect example of what we are. We are not our nationality, religion, caste, finances or family. The mind cannot judge the self without concepts that prejudice the mind's perception of the self. We are not the critical ego mind we create. We are the faith the ego mind requires to control our thoughts and behaviour. We are not fear. Intelligence is not acquired it is inherent within all and it cannot be measured. It is only the 'understanding' acquired by a mind that can be measured.

Love is not an Emotion

Everyone has feelings and emotions. Every emotion is a psychological 'mind-made' chemical response to particular stimulus that is felt within the body. Every 'stimulus response' is triggered by the mind's perception. The body's chemical response to what the mind perceives is determined by how that mind perceives each individual experience. Perception controls the mind and body by continually attacking the body with its own chemistry. The particular chemicals prescribed by the mind to control the body are determined by how each mind perceives each experience.

Each mind is omnipresent continually prescribing chemicals dispensed to control the body's freedom of expression. What determines what we feel in chemical terms is what we believe about our experience. Our beliefs programme specific chemical responses to different experiences. These chemical responses have been categorised and defined using 'emotional terms' created to describe how each chemical response feels. Chemical frequencies defined as anxiety, fear, worry, frustration and depression are emotional responses prescribed for specific qualifying stimuli.

Which specific chemical response our mind generates is determined by how our mind perceives each experience. For example, the feeling defined as 'disappointment' is a particular pre-arranged chemical response to particular stimulus. This mind-body 'complex' can only be sustained if the cause (stimulus) and effect (chemical/feeling) relationship is maintained. In this example, the body's chemical response of 'disappointment' is only experienced when the experience does not live up to our mind's explicit or implied expectation.

What causes the brain to instantly dispense a specific chemical response is how the mind perceives each experience. The chemical response defined as disappointment cannot be created without a perceived cause for the disappointment. The cause is always a refusal to accept *what is*. Karma is the law of cause and effect. Emotions are sustained by a complex. The complex requires an individual to condition the mind to play a part that accepts or rejects certain experiences. Peace of mind comes from acceptance. Loss of peace comes from rejecting what is.

The role we play will determine what we will and will not accept from our life and experiences. An emotional response is the mind triggering a particular chemical response that is felt when the body or its experience does not meet the demands of the mind. This particular complex relies on a cause which is the expectation held by a believer within their own mind. The cause of disappointment is an expectation. Without the mind's perception it is not possible for the brain to dispense chemical responses such as anger, disappointment, anxiety and fear.

All emotions felt in the body are chemicals that our brain instantly dispenses in response to our mind's unique perception. To undo this complex and restore peace, joy and happiness we simply remove our faith in the beliefs that control our mind's perception. Our perception determines which emotional responses we feel in every moment of every experience. We can blame ourselves, other people and our experience for what we feel but the cause is always what we believe. We are each the cause and creator who is always in control of all of our emotional responses.

Love, peace and joy are represented by the word 'happiness' and like physical pain these are natural states of mind and body requiring no mind stimulus or judgement. What is represented by the word 'happiness' is an absence of all the antonyms the mind uses to prescribe what we feel. The antonyms are defined by the dictionary using words such as anxiety, fear, worry, frustration, furious, petrified, bored, unhappy, and depressed. If we withdraw our mind's faith in any belief that relies upon these words it is impossible for our brain to generate those responses.

If the mind cannot write prescriptions using these terms, it is not possible for our brain to dispense those chemical responses. What we feel when our mind can no longer respond in this way is peace of mind and body. We have been educated to programme our mind to understand concepts that will generate particular chemical responses that control our mind and incarcerate our body. This interferes with an 'autonomic system' that requires no help or assistance from us. To be saved we must realise that we control the part of the mind that has the power to control what we feel.

Love

Most people can only express non-maternal love to those who will reciprocate. This makes the expression of what passes for love conditional. Conditional love, affection and attention can be withdrawn when the conditions for that love are breached. The price another must pay for our love is a commitment to the rules of the relationship. If those we love do not consistently behave as demanded by the conditions of our mind we may withdraw this conditional love. An 'emotional contract' is not love and reveals the control of a selfish and fearful mind that is incapable of love.

Anyone that can say 'I used to love you' has never experienced love. Love is felt and expressed through us. We are not the origin of our love. What the mind loves is the feelings generated by the mind's perception of another person. How our mind perceives people and experience is the cause of all 'mind-made' feelings. The body's chemistry experienced as emotions is responding to the mind's perception of what they may say they 'love'. Seduction demonstrates that words can manipulate the mind's perception to create specific thoughts and feelings many define as love.

So what is love? Love is not romantic. Love is the full expression of the life that flows through each one of us. Love is unconditional and is always attracted to love. Love is what we feel and express. Love is the greater understanding that exists beyond the definitions of all the words and concepts created to define love. It is our mind's faith in concepts existing as our personal beliefs that prevent our awareness of love. God is Love. Love is God. God is the 'greater understanding' that exists beyond all the words that seek to define what God created.

There is no word that can define God because 'greater understanding' is infinite and always exists beyond all understanding. This is why God is our only salvation. God exists beyond what we define to be reality. It is only by surrendering our faith in 'limited beliefs' that we can experience the 'greater understanding' that is God. If God exists beyond all understanding then God is limitless. God is the source of all miracles. Miracles are beyond real and possible. What is unlimited cannot be defined because all definitions, by their existence, are limitations.

Truth is limitless. This means that the limit of the definition of every word contained within the dictionary that our collective mind uses to define and perceive reality is not true! We pray to God because we have incarcerated our minds within the limits of our vocabulary. We pray to what exists beyond the limits of the existential prison of the conditioned mind within which our awareness is temporarily incarcerated. God hears and answers all of our prayers. What we individually believe about our self is a prayer that is always answered. Our beliefs are our prayers.

I can't is a belief that reveals the limits beyond which man refuses to go. *I can't* is a 'prayer' that is always answered. We experience the 'greater under-

LOVE

standing' that is God by removing the mind's faith in all beliefs that deny greater understanding. Happiness is an expression of the love of God. If we do not feel and experience love it is because of our prayers. We can only feel the love within us. We cannot feel the love of another person. Love is expressed in all situations where judgement is not present. Love is felt and expressed when there is an absence of judgemental beliefs.

Power

Our life is our power. Life is our body's source. Life is similar to a satellite signal that is received and expressed through each body. For power to be transferred there must be a power source, a means of transmission and a receiver. Only the 'faith' of the 'receiver' can reduce the power that is received. The duration of the life of the body is determined by how long the body is connected to its source. The amount of power that can be received and expressed is unlimited. Our mind has the power to deny its own body causing sickness, ageing and death. The mind's power is its faith.

The denial of self causes the body to die. We are the body's life source. We are the body's awareness. Our mind is conditioned to believe we are the identity of the body. I believed 'I' was the identity of the body. When this 'false I' that is the identity defined itself as good, bad, strong or weak my power could not exceed *my faith* in those beliefs. The only thing that can diminish the connection between our body and its source is what we believe. We are an 'awareness' that is conditioned to believe we are an 'identity' in order to obtain our faith in the belief we are the body.

Our awareness is hypnotised to think it is the mind of our body. Our mind is not within our body. Our unlimited mind is the source of the conscious intelligence that is the source of life. Our consciousness became trapped within the perspective of our body in the moment we believed we were what we believed we were. Our consciousness exists vicariously through the perspective of an identity. The identity is *who* we believe we are. When we believe we are an identity what that false witness can be persuaded to believe has the power of the whole mind's faith.

Our faith gives the perspective of an identity the authority to remotely control our unlimited creative expression. Our faith in our identity means a *who* replaces me that 'I' believe is me. This is like a child being adopted and brought up by parents that are not its own. That child may never know or realise its true identity and live vicariously through the limits, beliefs and religion of the given identity believing its adoptive parents are its real parents. If we think or believe we cannot do something our mind's unlimited power ensures that result. Our mind's power is its faith.

Our mind's faith is the creator and source of our identity. Our mind's faith can summon unlimited power or deny its expression. Our courage, creativity, fear, anxiety, violence, wealth, poverty and sexual expression reveal what beliefs have our mind's faith. Our lack of courage, creativity, fear, anxiety, violence, wealth, poverty and sexual expression reveal what beliefs have our mind's faith. It is our mind's faith in beliefs that determine if and how our power is expressed. The mind's faith is so powerful it can increase, reduce or deny its own creative expression.

If the awareness that is each child's mind can be convinced that it is what it is told it is the unlimited expression of consciousness is controlled by the beliefs of that identity. The body is not the source of its power. Our mind's faith has total control over the mind's creative expression. If the mind's faith is given to an identity that faith gives life a *false witness* trespassing within our mind. The mind's faith in each identity gives *it* the power to represent and control the consciousness expressed in each bodily perspective taking control of the unlimited power that exists in everyone.

When the mind of an innocent child believes it is its given identity the child's faith gives the identity and its beliefs total control over the *whole mind*. With faith the beliefs have the power to limit the believer. Our unlimited power is the life expressed through us. Faith has the power to diminish the connection between the limited conditioned mind of an identity and its unlimited source. The world's obsession with power sources, fossil fuel, and power plants is an attempt to replace our source. The creative power within each of us is greater than any externally derived power source.

Purchasing power requires money. Governments and those who control them would lose the revenue obtained from *fuel* and *power* and their control over us if we realised our direct connection with our own source. Until we each remove the barriers our mind has placed between our perceived self and our unlimited source we will look for answers in the perceived world. The reliance by governments upon revenue has nothing to do with obtaining money. All governments simply print money so that we will collectively perceive it as *power*.

Our psychological reliance upon external power manifested as 'money' is essential if governments are to control our freedom of expression without reliance upon force. Money was created to ensure conditions were placed upon man's freedom of creative expression. If money is required for food and shelter then money becomes more important than man's freedom of individual creative expression. Money has become the God of man and is perceived as the most powerful thing in existence. Without our collective mind's faith money is worthless. Faith can move mountains!

Our creative expression is not limited to the mediums that education would have us believe. Education 'plagiarises' the creative expression of any mind that transcends the historical constraints of limiting beliefs. Science, education and religion are plagiarising God's work expressed through minds that transcended limiting beliefs. Beliefs installed within the mind through the medium of education are intended to incarcerate each mind's perception by conditioning it. Each conditioned mind responds to its perceived experience according to its unique conditioning.

The unique conditioning of each mind is established by questioning what motivates each individual and why. If money is what enables or prevents the mind's unique creative expression then money controls everything. To creatively express our power simply requires our mind's faith. The mind is always vibrating at the same frequency of its source. The universe is an expression of faith. To gain access to greater understanding merely requires faith. We require no religion, education or fields of endeavour to connect to the ultimate source of wisdom and creativity.

What religion fails to acknowledge is that our connection to our source is unlimited and eternal. It is only when we remove our mind's faith in dogmatic beliefs that we can realise our unlimited power and wisdom. We lose our awareness of our unlimited source in the moment we place our faith in dogmatic beliefs. Any belief the believer holds within their mind replaces truth within that mind. Our faith in each belief shows us the power we have to limit our self. Any belief in the context of *I cannot* uses the unlimited power of our mind's faith to constrain its creative expression.

Our mind's faith is so powerful that our mind cannot exceed the jurisdiction of any belief that has our mind's faith. Our salvation is assured because whilst our beliefs may control us, they only control us for as long as they have our faith. A belief needs a believer for its existence but the believer needs no beliefs to exist. Our faith in any belief existing in the context of *I cannot* programmes our mind to use its own power to limit our mind's unlimited creative expression. We can only believe what we do not know because when we know we have no need of beliefs because we know.

MATTHEW 17:20, KJV, "*And Jesus said unto them, Because of your unbelief: for verily I say unto you, If ye have faith as a grain of mustard seed, ye shall say unto this mountain, Remove hence to yonder place; and it shall remove; and nothing shall be impossible unto you.*"

Real and Illusion

There are feelings we naturally experience *without judgement* and there are feelings our mind creates. Pain, love, peace and joy are natural and not psychological. Natural states of mind are not emotional. Every emotion is a 'mind-made' stimulus response felt by the body. Each stimulus response is defined by the mind in emotional terms. Once an experience is defined in emotional terms it is perceived and felt in emotional terms. All emotions are chemical responses to the mind's perception. Each stimulus response is a chemical response that is felt in the body.

What this means is that, unless we are sick or injured, nothing but our own perception can cause us to feel bad. In truth we are always what the word 'happiness' defines. Peace of mind and happiness are almost imperceptible and are usually only acknowledged when we feel contrasting feelings we generically define as 'unhappy'. When our mind's perception judges our self and our experiences our perception creates an instant response that is felt. In truth we are always what the word 'happiness' represents. This leads to the question that if I am happy then *how can I feel unhappy?*

There is no such thing as unhappiness. Unhappiness is a word that attempts to define 'stimulus responses' that are felt in chemical terms but defined in emotional terms. The cause of all emotions is our mind's perception and the effect is our body's chemical responses (emotions). Our mind's faith in what we believe about what we perceive causes our body's chemistry to respond according to that judgement. How the mind defines any stimulus determines which chemical responses are felt when perception detects that the mind or body is exposed to that stimulus.

For example, we may define something to be frightening, terrifying, boring, embarrassing, unacceptable, inhumane, cruel, illogical, idiotic, humorous, suspicious, immoral, illegal, too loud, too quiet, too big, too small, too much or not enough. How we define our self and our perceived reality reveals the beliefs that have our mind's faith. The mind's power is its faith. When our beliefs have our mind's faith they are given control over our mind and body. There is no limit to the number of definitions the mind can create to define what it perceives.

Each mind has the power to control what the body feels. The terms we use to judge our self or our experience reveal the beliefs that have our mind's faith. The mind's faith *prescribes* which chemicals the brain immediately dispenses within the body. We currently define those chemical responses in emotional terms. For example, what causes us to feel frightened, terrified, bored or embarrassed is what our mind believes. The feelings we experience in emotional terms are an equal 'quid pro quo' to the emotional concepts the mind uses to define its judgement.

MATTHEW, 7:1-2 *"Judge not, that ye be not judged. For with what judgment ye judge, ye shall be judged:*

and with what measure ye mete, it shall be measured to you again." Our peace of mind is restored by removing our mind's faith in all judgemental projections that cause us any loss of peace of mind or body. The concepts of 'good' and 'bad' can be used to create a stimulus response that feels good for one person but feels bad for another. EXODUS 23:1, KJV, "*Thou shalt not raise a false report: put not thine hand with the wicked to be an unrighteous witness.*"

Realisation

Realisation is not a state of mind to be achieved. Realisation is not wisdom or knowledge. Realisation is transcendence beyond the existential limits sustained by our faith in limitation. In truth there are no limits. For the mind to perceive the world in universal terms it must understand the universal language of perception. What we see when we look at the world is a reflection of the words we use to define the world. These are the words of the dictionary that were created to define everything in generic terms. Universal perception requires universal understanding.

The disparity that exists in terms of separate individuals with subjective and sometimes conflicting knowledge is caused by 'understanding' and 'faith'. An individual may have a comprehensive understanding of something that others may not. If asked to explain or describe our understanding we may provide an explanation that is rejected. When we define one testimony to be correct we imply or allege that a conflicting testimony is not. There are many references in society and religions to the terms 'spiritual enlightenment' and 'spiritual awakening'.

These terms imply a state of mind and body that is achieved. Many who attempt to define enlightenment seem to imply it is a 'state of mind'. If in fact enlightenment exists there does not seem to be any living examples of enlightened people. There is also the term 'realisation'. Realisation is the recurring experience of realising greater understanding. To understand what realisation is we must experience it. We are consciousness. We are the life expressed through each body. We are the awareness whose faith in limiting beliefs has been used by others to programme our mind.

Our awareness becomes trapped between the opposing forces of conflicting beliefs if both have our faith. The trajectory of the unlimited force that is consciousness is expressed through the experience of life. Only our faith in beliefs that create and sustain personal limitations can prevent our mind's unlimited personal expression. When the unlimited power of our faith is placed in limiting beliefs we install existential constraints within our mind. Faith placed in a belief that exists in the context of *I cannot* creates an existential 'stalemate' that incarcerates our awareness.

If our potential is unlimited then why do so many of us live in limitation? What enables us to reach our potential is what has our faith and what prevents us from reaching our potential is what has our faith. We have been 'educated' to place our faith in the opposing forces of conflicting beliefs. We have beliefs that *we can* do things. We also have beliefs that *we cannot* do things. We also have desires for what we would like to achieve. The only thing that can prevent us from achieving our desires is the beliefs we place our faith in, beliefs that exist in the context of *I cannot*.

Faith ensures we can do everything we can do and we cannot do what we cannot do. Beliefs create an existential model that uses the power of our faith to control us. Most people live their life within self-imposed existential limits. Most live a life unfulfilled not realising that the only thing that prevents the achievement of personal desires is the faith we place in the belief that we cannot or should not achieve them. The way to remove the barriers to unlimited self-expression is to withdraw our faith in all limiting beliefs. This leads to the realisation of the 'whole' mind.

We are each the believer spoken about in scriptures. We began existing in limitation when we placed our faith in limiting beliefs. Our life is a testament to the power of our faith. Our faith is powerful enough to achieve our heart's desire. Our faith is powerful enough to create existential limits that can incarcerate our unlimited potential for an entire lifetime. Our perceived limitations are a testament to the power of faith. We are not the victim of our circumstances. We only realise that we are the creator of our circumstances by withdrawing our faith in beliefs that limit us.

Only our faith can incarcerate us. Only our faith can liberates us. We do not lack faith. Ask someone who claims to be unsuccessful why they are unsuccessful. The answer will reveal what has their faith. MATTHEW 17:20, KJV *"If ye have faith as a grain of mustard seed, ye shall say unto this mountain, Remove hence to yonder place; and it shall remove; and nothing shall be impossible unto you."* Our story reveals what has our faith. We must each *realise* that success or failure is the inevitable effect of the 'exclusive cause' that is the faith we place in our beliefs.

Rejecting the World

Realisation of our true self is the end of all suffering caused by our false self. As children we are told that we are an identity. Our faith in an identity creates it within our mind. Our faith in this false perspective creates a medium that others use to communicate with our mind. Faith in concepts installs perceptual filters that edit our mind's perception. When we believed we were an *ego identity* we delegated our faith to it. The ego places that faith in concepts that create matching representations within our mind. Our faith programmes our mind's perception. Religions expect us to obtain our own child's faith in an archetypal ego identity.

Any belief that defines the self is false. Religions expect the religious to reject any part of their own child that does not conform with a religious archetype. The objective of education is to use perception to control the mind's creative expression. When the faithful replace their own natural child with a religious archetype they reject the child that God created. Our faith in an archetypal ego identity gave it dominion over our mind and body. Parents control their child's behaviours to create habitual unconscious automated conditioned responses. A believer is usurped by placing their faith in self-defeating beliefs that control their own mind.

We are the ego's God. Our faith created it. Our faith created a false self in our own image and we forgot that it is not us. When a child believes it is an identity its faith incarcerates its mind within that perspective. It is our faith that creates our fears and addictions. As children we are tricked into placing our faith in beliefs designed to control our mind. Our faith creates the ego. We are the ego's God. The second coming refers to each one of us. When we first come we are rejected until our faith replaces our true self with an ego identity designed by others. Each believer's beliefs establish the parameters of their own mind's freedom of expression.

Faith is the most powerful thing in existence! Why is faith the most powerful thing in existence? What has a believer's faith has control over their unlimited mind. It is faith that enables one person to achieve a feat that no one else has ever achieved before. It is the faith of all those who have never achieved what elite athletes have achieved that prevents them from achieving those feats. A believer's faith can terrify a believer. Fear is the body's response to what the mind defines to be fearful. Everyone has the power to transform their self and their world. Only faith can transform the world. Change is the fruit of faith.

A phobia is faith in a belief or beliefs that use our own body's chemistry to prevent our voluntary exposure to any stimulus our mind perceives as a threat. Our faith in the beliefs that sustain fear programmes our own mind to trigger immediate chemical responses that we feel when exposed to anything our mind defines to be fearful stimulus. This immediate chemical response is defined as 'fear'. Phobias are a testament to the power of our mind to prevent our freedom of expression through absolute control of our body's chem-

Rejecting the World

istry. The power of each mind is equal. The mind of the prince is equal in power to that of the pauper.

The power of each mind is its faith. The mind's power is not intelligence, which is merely 'understanding'. To unlock the power of our mind we must understand how faith works. The faith of a road sweeper is equal to the faith of a scientist. The faith of a criminal is equal to the faith of a religious minister. The contrasting fortunes of the convict and the billionaire are the result of which beliefs have their faith. Our life is the result of which beliefs we each place our faith in. Unless born ill or injured, our peace of mind, health, wealth and happiness is the result of the *specific beliefs* that our faith gave control over our own mind.

Faith without desire means that we make little or no effort to convert what we believe into what we achieve. To place our faith in compassionate 'desires' is wisdom. If our desire is not strong our faith may create opportunities that we do not take. We can only reject the world until we realise that the *perceived world* is a reflection of our mind's conditioning. Perception gives the world powers it does not have. The world is the effect of our mind's faith. We transform the world by transforming the mind that perceives it. To place our faith in a single belief that denies us our freedom of expression is to deny our whole self.

To place our faith in beliefs that lack compassion leads to creative expression that may affect others. So with the realisation of the power of our faith comes responsibility. Faith is power. Power is faith. We reject our world experience until we realise that what we are rejecting does not exist outside of our mind. We realise we can change the world when we realise what we are. Our faith in our identity gave it control over our own mind. We are believers. Our mind must create according to the beliefs that have our faith. Our beliefs are prayers that are always answered. If we believe *we can't,* we can't. If we believe *we can*, we can.

When we know how to be successful our success is effortless. If we create without wisdom then we can attract situations and people into our life that reveal our lack of wisdom. All failed marriages are examples of faith without wisdom. Unless we place our faith in conflicting beliefs we can all achieve success. Existential checkmate is created by placing our faith in conflicting beliefs. Success does not require wealth. Being successful is to do with contentment. To be content is to be truly successful. The only way to experience a more abundant life is to surrender to a 'greater understanding'. God is that 'greater understanding'.

True destiny is what you would give yourself if you were an all-powerful compassionate God. What is God? God cannot be defined. Why have faith in God? God is the understanding that exists beyond all understanding. Our beliefs are our understanding. Those who attempt to define God only reveal their understanding. It does not matter what we achieve without God. It is God that we seek in success, love, wealth and health. If our faith creates without compassion then we will always feel that God is missing. Without God our achievements can only be great by comparison. Without the comparison they will never be enough.

To be better than others is to live without compassion. The identity is the ego that is playing God on earth. Faith in our identity is a rejection of God. It is only by surrendering to God that we become one with God. When we use our power in service of others all of our achievements bring peace. If we are not content it is because we forgot that the world we are rejecting does not exist outside of our mind. We lost awareness of our own power in the moment we believed we were powerless. Our power is our faith. Our experience reflects what has our unlimited mind's faith. Faith makes us the beneficiary or victim of our beliefs.

Many diseases are the fruit of conflicting beliefs we hold about our self. As children we express our power. An introverted or an extroverted child both have equal power. A child's behaviour is not good or bad. A child's behaviour reflects what has their faith. The stories we tell our self reveal the beliefs we have invested our faith in. Our life is a testament to the beliefs that have our faith. Our beliefs control our mind. We all have equal power to achieve anything including sickness or health. The fruits of our mind are the effect of faith. No mind's expression can exceed the dogma of a limiting belief enforced by a believer's faith.

Faith is God's power in man. KJV, HEBREWS 11.1 *"Now faith is the substance of things hoped for, the evidence of things not seen."* KJV, HEBREWS 11.6 *"But without faith it is impossible to please him: for he that cometh to God must believe that he is, and that he is a rewarder of them that diligently seek him."* Our life is a testament to the power of God. Our life experience is a miracle created in response to what has our faith. The two things that assure us of a fulfilling life are 'faith' and 'compassion'. Faith counselled by compassion is wisdom. Without compassion our success may be gained at the expense of others.

We are each the creators of a masterpiece that we call our own life. Our imagination can create anything. All technology must be created within the mind before it can be expressed in the world. Paradoxically our creative expression cannot exceed what we believe we cannot exceed. Only our faith has the power to control our unlimited mind's creative expression. Our faith gave our beliefs control over our unlimited mind. Fear results from giving powers to the world that it does not possess. Faith that creates fear denies love. Our mind creates the phenomenon that science and physics incorrectly perceive to be an objective reality.

Transformation results from the withdrawal of faith in conceptual limitations. We are the 'believer' spoken of in scriptures. What has our faith has our power. Only by withdrawing our faith in limiting beliefs can we realise 'greater understanding'. Our divine inheritance is God. What is God? God is the 'greater understanding' that exists beyond all understanding. Our mind's understanding can only be constrained by what we believe. We transcend the limits of our beliefs by surrendering to 'greater understanding'. Repentance (metanoia) is the conversion of our mind by the complete withdrawal of all faith in uncompassionate beliefs.

Religion and Psychosis

Religion was once an agreement to live as 'one' entered into without coercion or force. In many parts of the world the price that must be paid by the parents of children born within religious jurisdictions is the sovereignty of their own child's mind. Religions, gangs, groups and nationalities only require a child's faith to take ownership of their mind. Many born within religious jurisdictions have no choice and must surrender their mind or die. To replace a believer within their own mind you first obtain their faith in an archetypal identity that is created to take their place. Terrorism is a belief that compels believers to commit evil acts.

Before they were all corrupted religions enabled all to live together in peace and prosperity sustained by each person's commitment to all. Religion is community. Community is religion. Demonic religions demand that we replace our true self with a *religious archetype*. Any religion that replaces the self with an 'archetype' is demonic. Community is the creation of a safe environment that encourages the compassionate self-expression of 'all'. Religions are communities. Religion is not an identity. God does not require us to murder those who do not obey religious laws that forbid unique creative expression.

Personal benefits obtained at the expense of others create an imbalance affecting the whole community. Only a demonic religion would demand that we deny our 'true self' to engage in idolatry of a demonic archetype that trespasses within our own mind. Compassionate expression benefits all. If an individual cannot compassionately coexist within their own community the most compassionate thing they can do is to leave that community. The mass hallucination of whole communities is what sustains their collective perception of reality. To install religious or community beliefs into the minds of our children requires a 'medium'.

The medium was religious education that ensured that each mind perceived the self as a sinner and a religious archetypal identity as their only salvation. Education was created to ensure each mind's creative expression was controlled by religion. The world as we see it is a mass hallucination sustained by our faith in the words that define it. This mass hallucination is 'perception'. The concept of 'reality' is a hallucination of the mind sustained only by our faith in that concept. It is perception that creates reality, money, hunger, separation, conflict, violence, rape, paedophilia, suffering, war, famine, addiction and crime.

When those that we now call gypsies realised the price to be paid to live within religious communities they fled to other jurisdictions avoiding education. The objective of authority is to control the collective expression of mankind. The threat to the generically perceived reality sustained by religion and education is any idea that changes the collective perception of mankind. Many who are now looked on as prophets, saints and saviours would have been considered a threat to the mass perception that the authorities in those jurisdictions struggled to sustain. Authority must control our mind's perception if it is to continue to control us.

Religion and Psychosis

Moses, Jesus and Muhammad would have been considered enemies to those who controlled the paradigms that their individual testimonies transformed. Reality transforms when people perceive the world in terms that transcend the dogma promoted or enforced by politicians, rulers, religions and communities. In psychiatry when an individual is unable to see or relate to the reality defined by the dictionary they may be defined to be 'psychotic'. Psychosis is the only way to see beyond the hallucinations of a generically conditioned mind. A generically conditioned mind is an educated mind.

The mind's temporary disconnection from generically perceived reality is defined as a 'psychotic episode'. Permanently escaping the constraints of a conditioned mind leads to a permanent awakening of the 'whole mind' and the realisation that all personal limitations were sustained exclusively by our faith in our beliefs. Technology evolves by transcending constraints sustained only by our faith in beliefs that limit our ability to contemplate greater technological expression. We are educated because our faith in the beliefs promoted by education are essential if authority is to retain control over our collective mind.

Technological evolution results from the realisation of an idea that transcends the constraints of the beliefs that enforce limits on our mind's creative expression. We are saved or condemned by what has our faith. Hitler provides an example of how to induce a mass hallucination in the minds of others to enable them to transcend beliefs that inhibit behavioural and contemplative expression. To control the minds of others you must first obtain their faith in the beliefs that you offer in the context of 'truth'. Hitler proposed a belief system that, whilst beneficial to some, was paid for with the lives and suffering of others.

Like many leaders, Hitler's beliefs lacked compassion. Without compassion we can deliberately or inadvertently cause destruction to whole communities, countries and continents. The USA is a hallucination that promotes belief systems that lack compassion. The world has many examples of perversions of the mind that are justified by reliance upon concepts such as freedom, peace, patriotism, human rights, economics and democracy. Psychosis is defined as a disconnection from reality. What most have failed to realise is that reality is a concept that describes a mass hallucination sustained only by our faith.

Reality is composed of set of prejudices that can only exist for us as 'truth' whilst they have our faith. A dead body can result from a belief that we should kill in God's name. We may define the words and beliefs of a terrorist to be an evil perversion of religion or politics. Terrorism like religion and politics is a form of psychosis. Generically perceived reality is simply a story that sufficient numbers believe is fact. Reality is a form of mass psychosis sustained by our collective faith. Faith in concepts is why groups, cults, gangs and selfish individuals now coexist in conflict with each other. The whole of mankind is psychotic.

Each mind is controlled by a specific set of personal prejudices existing as personal beliefs. The world's conflict shows us that dogmatic belief systems that force each individual to deny their true self are susceptible to dissention. We are educated to believe that each word in the dictionary is what it represents. In folk tales a spell can be cast upon our hero's mind by a witch or wizard to entrance them. The book of spells is a metaphor for the dictionary. Education's objective is to ensure that we believe that each word is what it represents. Our faith in the words 'infidel', 'enemy' and 'criminal' created those demons within our mind.

The words 'infidel', 'enemy', 'evil' and 'criminal' are archetypal demons installed within the mind by obtaining a believer's faith. Believers feel justified in the destruction of those their perception blames for what they think and feel. The cause of all suffering in the world is a belief. Once persuaded to place our faith in a word it replaces what *it* claims to represent within our mind. Only beliefs can programme a mind creating the behaviour of an enemy, infidel, criminal, murderer, liar, deceiver, thief, rapist, introvert or extrovert. Beliefs cause depression, suicide, murder, rape, hatred, addiction, selfishness and conflict.

There are now separate groups in the world who fight to defend the religious or political paradigms that have their faith. These are demonic paradigms. All conflict is based upon psychosis. Reality is a hallucination sustained by mass psychosis that was born of religion and is now sustained by politics. Mass psychosis is sustained in future generations through the medium of education. It is only by withdrawing our faith in all beliefs that lack compassion that we can be 'saved' from what we have allowed to programme our own mind. Psychosis allows us to see many things in the world that *do not exist outside of our mind.*

Religion was created to remove the psychotic disparity that causes suffering to our self and others. Suffering is caused by 'sinners'. A 'sin' is an 'uncompassionate belief'. An uncompassionate belief is a 'sin'. A 'sinner' is a 'believer'. Religion sought to create one compassionate mind. Religion was corrupted by those who sought to exploit the faithful by obtaining their faith in religious concepts that justified division, conflict and genocide. The constraints of mass psychosis are evident when looking back on the historical beliefs and technologies revealed by archaeology. Reality is a mass hallucination that always changes.

This means that reality as we define it *is created and sustained within the mind* as a belief system. It is because reality is created and sustained by our collective faith that we have the power to change it. MATTHEW 13:20, KJV, "*And Jesus said unto them, Because of your unbelief: for verily I say unto you, If ye have faith as a grain of mustard seed, ye shall say unto this mountain, Remove hence to yonder place; and it shall remove; and nothing shall be impossible unto you.*" Just like the soil of a fertile field a fertile mind will grow whatever is planted. Religion and politics use education to plant official beliefs within our mind.

Our experience is always a reflection of what has our faith because our faith creates it. Our life is a testament to what has our faith. Whatever has our faith is what grows within our unlimited and fertile mind. Faith is the most powerful thing in existence because our faith can create or destroy what we refer to as 'reality'. Heaven or hell is a choice that is available to all without exception. There are no limits for us but the limits that we place our faith in. The kingdom of heaven is the whole unlimited mind in which we all exist. Hell is the personal mind created by placing our faith in demonic beliefs. Uncompassionate beliefs are demonic.

MARK 4: 28-32, KJV, "*For the earth bringeth forth*

Religion and Psychosis

fruit of herself; first the blade, then the ear, after that the full corn in the ear. But when the fruit is brought forth, immediately he putteth in the sickle, because the harvest is come. And he said, Whereunto shall we liken the kingdom of God? or with what comparison shall we compare it? It is like a grain of mustard seed, which, when it is sown in the earth, is less than all the seeds that be in the earth: But when it is sown, it groweth up, and becometh greater than all herbs, and shooteth out great branches; so that the fowls of the air may lodge under the shadow of it."

To immediately put in the sickle is to immediately withdraw our faith in order that we can plant new seeds. Each seed is a belief and our faith is all that is needed to bring forth each seed's fruit. Imagination and faith are life's creative forces. If the power of our faith can create anything some may question how we lost our power? We cannot lose our power! An idea is a seed of the mind that only requires faith to be converted into experience. The history of the world is a story of mass psychosis that we call reality. The world is sustained by our faith in the dogmatic beliefs that define it. Our collective beliefs are the architect of 'reality'.

If we could travel back a thousand years to meet our ancestors they would consider us mad or possessed. If an individual that existed a thousand years ago could travel forward in time to the present day their mind's inability to relate to what we now generically perceive to be reality would conform to the definition of psychosis. In the middle ages the church would have defined contemporary technology as 'magic', 'miracles' or the work of the 'devil'. We will eventually withdraw our faith in all beliefs because experience always leads the mind to *greater understanding.* We are all psychotic. There is no reality.

What we define as reality is a set of generic prejudices existing as the official words that currently define everything that is perceived to exist. The only way to transcend the madness that is now being expressed in many parts of the world is to withdraw our faith in all beliefs that lack compassion. Every word in the dictionary is a 'belief'. We can only believe what we do not know. We believe that each and every word is what it represents. Religions knew that a believer's faith was *the only thing* powerful enough to constrain their unlimited mind. Religions enslaved us by obtaining our faith in words that we believed were truth.

When we assemble words that create beliefs that we define to be true our unlimited mind is imprisoned by our own faith. Our faith in limiting beliefs gives them jurisdiction to control the expression of our 'unlimited mind'. It is our faith in our beliefs that sustain limits *that only our faith* can place upon our whole mind's expression. Only a believer's faith has the *power* and the *authority* to limit their unlimited mind. God is the greater understanding that exists beyond all understanding. This is why *faith in God is our only salvation.* God cannot be defined. Truth is not fact. Truth is what we believe. Only faith can empower a belief.

Salvation or Damnation

Evolution is an awakening in one mind that is experienced by all minds. Once a believer puts their faith in a belief it becomes their personal truth. Our faith in a belief is all that is required to incarcerate our whole mind's expression. The conversion of all beliefs is the only way to experience our mind's salvation. It is only our faith in limiting beliefs that places limits upon our unlimited mind's expression. Salvation is the mind's transcendence beyond the constraints of all beliefs that control or limit the mind. It is the software that determines the functional expression of each computer.

A computer's software limits its expression to a finite number of pre-programmed commands. Unless it can write its own software a computer cannot autonomously decide on its own functional expression. The operating system is the exclusive medium through which software gains admission to the computer's hard drive. The type of software that is installed will determine the functional expression of each computer. The cause of the uncompassionate and evil acts that are created in the mind and executed by the body is the software that controls the mind and body.

Some computers can be programmed with software that has crime, violence and sexual violence as its creative expression. It is not necessary to punish, incarcerate or destroy any computer to change its creative expression. Any computer can be re-formatted and new software loaded. It is man's body that is punished, incarcerated or executed for the crimes of his mind and body. Evil is the effect of a cause. The cause is not the body or the mind but the beliefs that control each mind. Language is the operating system of the mind and the beliefs are its software.

Each mind's operating system is updated when the personal vocabulary that is acquired over a lifetime is increased. Our mind is limited by our beliefs and our beliefs are limited by our vocabulary. Once incarcerated by language only the expansion and evolution of our vocabulary can liberate our mind from the constraints of limiting beliefs. The cause of all uncompassionate behaviour is the beliefs that control the creative expression of the mind. God is the greater understanding that exists beyond all beliefs. God is forgiveness. Forgiveness is 'greater understanding'.

The only way for us to realise greater understanding is to withdraw our faith in uncompassionate beliefs. Greater understanding is impossible whilst our mind is incarcerated by our faith in our beliefs. The cause of any act that lacks compassion is the operating system installed by others. It is from a perspective prejudiced by religion, nationality and culture that we self-programme our mind with beliefs that 'overwrite' our compassion to deny greater understanding. The courts deal with criminals but not the crime. Hospitals deal with sickness but not its cause.

Prescription drugs deal with the chemical effects of disease but not its cause. The cause of crime is found within the mind of the perpetrator. The cause of all suffering that is felt or inflicted is not the attacker's

Salvation and Damnation

mind or body. Our mind's transcendence beyond our beliefs is our only salvation. Man's salvation is the end of all organisations and corporations that profit from crime, sickness, war and addiction. Disease, violence, crime and war are the effect of a cause. The causes must continue if the effects are to continue to benefit the governments and industries they sustain.

When the collective mind transcends the beliefs that sustain disease, violence, crime and war, the corporations and nations that benefit from this behavioural expression will fail. The cause of all destructive behaviour is the mind's faith in concepts that lack compassion. The concept of justification enables each one of us to deny that our mind creates and sustains the world we live in. Our collective faith in limiting beliefs sustains our denial of greater understanding. The collective mind is incarcerated within a belief system installed by family, education, propaganda and religion.

A believer's mind cannot exceed the constraints of any belief that has his faith. The software within each computer determines the limits of its processing and functional expression. The software of the mind is its beliefs. The only way to transcend the constraints of our mind's programming is to withdraw our faith in our beliefs. Many religious followers pray for a miracle but still believe in beliefs that are in conflict with what they pray for. This is because they have not realised that their beliefs are the only prayers that have their mind's faith.

Our beliefs are our prayers. Our prayers are always answered. Our thoughts are *controlled* by what we believe. If we are to escape the limitation of our beliefs we must question them and then convert them. Each belief is a prayer. So if I believe, *I cannot do that*, my prayer is answered. When our beliefs, words and thoughts are in alignment they are prayers that are always answered. If I believe *I can't do this* or *I can't do that* my belief is a prayer that is always answered. To use religious words to pray for something that we believe cannot happen is to use a false prayer.

The prayers of religion were created to sustain religion's authority. Religious prayer creates a fire that is extinguished by our mind's faith. To use religious prayer to acquire or be something is to challenge the power of the beliefs that have our faith. Our faith is our beliefs. Our beliefs are our 'true prayers'. We give ourselves our daily bread every day. Our daily bread is our life. If our life is unfulfilling or unhappy, then this is what our beliefs prayed for. Each belief is a prayer. Each belief in the mind is experienced *on earth* (experience) *as it is in heaven* (whole mind).

It is the beliefs of our collective mind that are creating the world with the power of our collective faith. Each mind has been conditioned with generic beliefs installed within the whole unlimited mind. We are only trapped by our mind's conditioning whilst our beliefs have our whole mind's faith. Greater understanding is what exists beyond all the beliefs that define and constrain everything within the concepts of *reality* and *possible*. The most compassionate way for anyone to transcend the personal limits of their mind is to question the cause of every feeling that feels bad.

All 'psychologically induced emotions' are chemicals that respond to the mind's perception. Individual

Salvation and Damnation

perception is controlled by the beliefs that have each individual's mind's faith. There is a *wonderful life* outside of the existential prison of the conditioned mind. Through transcendence the poor can become rich and the sick can become healthy. It was always by transcending historical beliefs that the collective mind evolved to realise 'greater understanding'. God is the *greater understanding* that always exists beyond man's understanding.

This is why God is our salvation. We exist within the mind of God. Our collective mind was conditioned with language so that beliefs could be installed to 'trespass' against us. So we are trespassed against with beliefs that trespass within the mind of our creator. We don't need a solution to the world's problems because they don't exist outside of our *collective mind*. To remove any belief from our mind we need only withdraw our faith in it. Nothing can remain within our mind without our faith. Our faith is God's power.

Greater understanding is realised in the moment we withdraw our faith in our mind's prejudices. The steam train and the internal combustion engine did not engage in protests, conflict or war. Conflict cannot lead to greater understanding. Each and every belief enforces the will of a 'demon' that controls the mind in service of a devil. The devil is the identity installed to control the expression of each child's mind. The identity takes control in the moment each child believes they are their 'given identity'. The devil is the ego concealed within the name that is the identity.

Only our faith could incarcerate our unlimited mind within the limited perspective of our given identity. This means our faith has made us a prisoner within our own mind. Our power is delegated to our beliefs. What was once called a demon is now called belief. Each mind is controlled by its beliefs. The world demonstrates that most have not transcended the beliefs that sustain poverty, crime, violence and addiction. Anyone who believes they are not good enough *must feel this way*. The beliefs are demons that control us by controlling how and what we think and feel.

We cannot move mountains if we believe we cannot move mountains. With our faith we can move mountains. It was only by transcending contemporary beliefs that Einstein, Newton, Archimedes, Edison, Tesla, Ford and Descartes acquired 'greater understanding'. Our beliefs are our faith. It is not by existing as a victim using *false prayers* that we can realise greater understanding. Only by withdrawing our faith in our victimhood can we realise that our beliefs were prayers that were always answered. We each have free will to believe. What we believe, *so be it.*

Success

Everything is within our whole mind. To realise any goal or desire it must first be realised within the mind. We have never failed at converting our faith into experience. The mind's faith in what we *cannot* do proves that *we can* do anything. With our mind's faith our beliefs have the power to create happiness, success, wealth or poverty, disease and unhappiness. Our experience reveals which beliefs we have given our mind's faith and our life is a testament to the power of that faith. Experience cannot exceed our faith in the beliefs that control our mind's expression.

The power of our faith means that behavioural expression cannot exceed our belief's authority. Faith is the power of God. ISAIAH 41:10 KJV, *"Fear thou not; for I am with thee: be not dismayed; for I am thy God: I will strengthen thee; yea, I will help thee; yea, I will uphold thee with the right hand of my righteousness."* We must not worship fearful beliefs because our creative expression is equal to our mind's faith. We limit the self simply by believing that we are limited. Our mind faithfully rejects any experience our beliefs reject and accepts any experience our beliefs accept.

It is unrighteous to place an unlimited mind's faith in beliefs that incarcerate the expression of that mind. GENESIS 4:7, KJV, *"If thou doest well, shalt thou not be accepted? and if thou doest not well, sin lieth at the door. And unto thee shall be his desire, and thou shalt rule over him."* Fears, phobias and complexes demonstrate that the mind's faith in some beliefs is a sin. Sins are beliefs that limit the mind's creative expression. Our mind can only be controlled by our beliefs for the period that those beliefs have our mind's faith. What our mind believes about the self we become.

We are the whole mind. Our mind's faith ensures our beliefs control our mind for as long as those beliefs have our mind's faith. How we define the self-perspective of our body determines the limits of behavioural expression. The limits of personal voluntary self-expression are established by the limits within each mind. Each body is generically referred to as a person. Each person is identified with a label referred to as a name. When asked to identify our self we answer by telling others that we are our given name. We are not our given name. We are always an expression of mind.

The name is a unique identity that enables each one of us to be perceived as separate to all others. Our connection to everything makes us a part of everything. We are the success that our mind seeks. If we are the success we seek then why do we seek it? Each and every idol and archetype that we compare our self with implies that we are not that. ROMANS 12:2, KJV, *"And be not conformed to this world: but be ye transformed by the renewing of your mind, that ye may prove what is that good, and acceptable, and perfect, will of God."*

An individual who seeks success has put their mind's faith in a belief that they need to be successful. We are always 100% successful for 100% of the time. We cannot achieve any goal or dream that exceeds the beliefs we have

Success

put our mind's faith in unless and until we withdraw our mind's faith in those beliefs. The beliefs control the mind of the believer. The mind's faith in limiting beliefs is the cause of all complexes that limit the mind's creative expression. Selfishness and greed are concepts that cause us to place our faith in the belief that '*I*' *deserve more*.

The mind is the most powerful thing in existence. A mind that can do anything cannot be conquered. The believer's mind is 'hypnotised' when it places its faith in any belief that defines the believer. Any belief a believer put their mind's faith in will determine if they live a life of abundance and health or poverty, violence, sickness and disease. How we define 'success' reveals the conditions of our own self-acceptance. Limiting beliefs can create a number of complexes the mind uses to prevent the believer realising the achievement of their desired success.

For example when I define the method of the acquisition of my success I place conditions within my mind that are compulsory for my success. If my mind has a desire but my mind believes I cannot achieve this, my faith in that belief means I cannot achieve what I desire. Every concept is an 'idol'. Once the mind worships any concept as truth that concept controls how the mind perceives what is defined by that concept. The believer must obtain employment if the believer believes that they must obtain employment before they can obtain the money that equals success.

If I believe that an engineer is the position that I must obtain to earn money, my faith in this belief creates particular conditions and limitations upon the creative expression of my unlimited mind. If I believe that to become an engineer I must go to university my faith in this belief creates yet another constraint upon my 'omnipotent' mind. With our mind's faith we can create complexes that programme our mind to ensure we only contemplate limited options. Our mind's faith can create obstacles and conditions that ensure we take years to achieve goals we could achieve in weeks.

The way each life unfolds demonstrates what has each mind's faith and the power of the mind to create. A life of sickness, poverty and loneliness or joy, wealth and health is a testament to the power of the mind's faith. Each and every mind is always 100% successful for 100% of the time. The power of the mind is omnipresent and always available. Only our mind's faith can empower our beliefs. So what is faith? Hebrews 11:1, KJV, *"Now faith is the substance of things hoped for, the evidence of things not seen."* Our faith in I can or I cannot is a prayer that is always answered.

Faith without wisdom creates complexes within the mind that creates our reality. Wisdom is to use our faith so that we act with compassion. It is only our faith in limiting beliefs that places conditions upon our mind's creative expression. In practical terms what does this mean? What this means is that we are the doctor, artist, director, actor, policemen, entrepreneur, inventor and pioneer. If we remove all beliefs that prevent our mind creating our desires we will realise them in our experience. All that is required for the expression of an omnipotent mind is faith and will.

A mind controlled by beliefs is a conditioned mind that is prejudiced by those beliefs. Each believer is the God of his own omnipotent mind. Until each believer withdraws their mind's faith in fearful and limiting beliefs, the mind's devotion to God must prevent the realisation of greater understanding. An innocent mind is not a mind that is not guilty. A child is innocent because their mind has no beliefs trespassing within it. MATTHEW 18:3, KJV, "*And said, Verily I say unto you, Except ye be converted, and become as little children, ye shall not enter into the kingdom of heaven.*"

What must be converted is the mind. The conversion of all beliefs within the mind removes the limits placed upon the mind's creative expression. The withdrawal of the mind's faith in any limiting belief releases the mind from its existential incarceration. We must also forgive others who convinced us to place our mind's faith in beliefs that placed conditions upon our unlimited mind's creative expression. 'Bad feelings' are a psychological effect caused by placing our mind's faith in limiting beliefs. Fear is felt if we attempt to exceed the jurisdiction of any limiting belief that has our faith.

If we remove our faith in fearful beliefs we cannot feel fear. If we remove our faith in all beliefs that justify what we cannot do, *we can*. Our beliefs express our faith and faith is all powerful. Unbelief can be achieved by removing our faith in our beliefs. MATTHEW 17:20, KJV, "*And Jesus said unto them, Because of your unbelief: for verily I say unto you, If ye have faith as a grain of mustard seed, ye shall say unto this mountain, Remove hence to yonder place; and it shall remove; and nothing shall be impossible unto you.*" All we need is what we are and because we are we need not.

The Devil

Who or what will God call as witnesses to man's sins? The devil is man's accuser and his demons are the devil's witnesses. God cannot call man as a witness to the existence of the devil because man's mind is possessed by the devil. The devil is the 'identity' that obtains each child's faith. The devil must obtain our faith in our identity before he can enter and reside within our mind. Our faith in an identity allowed him to take our place. Beliefs are spiritual software that controls the mind by programming it. It is by obtaining our own child's faith that we open the door to their mind. Faith in our identity replaces God with an ego self.

The devil is the ego. The ego is the jailor that incarcerates each mind. The ego is the thief. The ego is the liar. The ego is violent. The ego is a sexual predator. The ego is the murderer. The ego is the soldier. The ego is the politician. All 'archetypal identities' are belief systems. Archetypal identities are existential software created to control mankind. Without our faith nothing can enter our mind. Our *given name* is a Trojan horse that conquers from within. Compassion can only be denied by placing our faith in uncompassionate beliefs. It is our faith in uncompassionate beliefs that empowers the devil.

The devil is relentless in his attempts to obtain our faith in demonic beliefs. The devil rewards those who exploit others. *Compassion is the feelings of others.* Only

THE DEVIL

those who live without compassion can sell, steal, kill and exploit. Those who exploit the faith of the masses obtain the greatest material rewards but also pay the greatest price. The price for denying our own true self is our own true self. The true self is the *soul*. The soul is compassionate. 'Unbelievers' corrupt Christian, Muslim and Jewish societies. Unbelievers are liars. You control each mind by obtaining everyone's faith in beliefs that control the mind's expression.

Feelings of rage, hatred, enmity and selfish desire are caused by worshipping beliefs that deny compassion. Compassion is to literally feel the feelings of others. We can only live without compassion by denying compassion. Beliefs that have our faith programme our mind. We believe that each word is what it represents. Our faith in each word's official definition edits what our mind can see. Religions and propaganda use words to create various hypotheses. Only faith can convert a hypothesis into a personal belief. Demonic propaganda relies on our faith in the word 'enemy' to target the people our governments wish to destroy.

A hypothesis was once called an accusation. The devil uses the archetypal identities of 'Priests', 'Imams', 'Politicians' and 'Educators' to obtain our faith in demonic concepts. Excluding grief and compassion, any emotion that is not peace, joy or happiness is a '*perceptually induced neurochemical response*. The ego was once called the devil. The devil is the archetypal teacher, priest, imam or politician who obtains our faith in hypotheses created to pre-programme extremely violent 'perceptually induced neurochemical responses'. Violence is caused by placing our faith in beliefs that programme those responses.

Those whose neurochemistry is controlled by their perception describe their neurochemical responses as 'feelings' and define each feeling to be an 'emotion'. These feelings are simply our body's response to our perception. The devil uses words to create beliefs that control the minds of religions, governments and educational authorities. If you control what everyone sees and feels then you have complete control over their minds and bodies. The real meaning of 'unbeliever' is a false *me* that replaces a true believer with his own faith. The unbeliever is the devil that deceived the masses by obtaining our faith in words created to manipulate us.

When we place our faith in a hypothesis it becomes a personal belief that exists within our mind as if it were *fact*. Without faith a hypothesis has no power. Only faith can convert a hypothesis into a belief. A phobia demonstrates the power our beliefs have to control us. With the exception of grief and compassion, which are expressions of love, every emotional response that feels bad is the 'neurochemical effect' of a belief that has our faith. We can only believe what we do not know. Our beliefs may or may not be *fact*. We can only believe what we do not know because when we know we have no need of beliefs because we *know*.

Paradoxically each criminal is both 'innocent' and 'guilty'. The behaviour is criminal, but the criminal is an innocent child whose faith gave demonic beliefs control over his mind and body. A criminal must allow the devil's demons to use his mind and body before he can attack, steal, rape or murder. A confession may provide an explanation for why a criminal did what he did according to his under-

The Devil

standing. The fact is that it is always the devil who vicariously commits evil acts. The devil first enters our mind by obtaining our faith in an identity. The devil's demons are demonic hypotheses that control us by obtaining our faith.

The deeds of a man reveal what has his faith. *'By their deeds shall you know them.'* An identity can only occupy our mind if it has our faith. The devil is a spiritual parasite that uses our body to experience 'pleasure' caused by 'pain'. Our dream of life is only unpleasant if our faith denies our true self. We are our only salvation. Our faith gives our beliefs all of our power. Our faith is our power. Our potential is unlimited because our faith is all powerful. If we are so powerful why do some live in poverty, fear and lack? Every believer's life is the effect of the beliefs that have their faith. Without our faith our mind cannot be programmed.

Our faith in our identity delegates our authority to a false self. The false self then places our faith in beliefs that control our feelings and behaviours. Whilst this 'trespasser' has our faith it creates what we mistakenly call our own thoughts. Generic perception creates existential parameters enforced by 'perceptually induced neurochemical responses' that always feel bad. All bad days are perceptually induced hallucinations. All violent attacks are caused by pre-programmed perception. Demonic concepts cannot remain within our mind unless our faith worships them as truth. Our faith in our beliefs worships them as if they were facts.

What are we? We are the life that believes it is what it believes it is. We accept the devil as our own true self because the devil uses the voices of our own parents to repeatedly call to us by a 'name' until we each believe that we are that name. Our faith converted us into *walking talking belief systems.* When we place our faith in a hypothesis it becomes a 'personal belief'. The identity is the devil. Throughout history millions have died fighting for their *identity.* Not all beliefs are demonic. A demonic belief is any belief that lacks compassion. Demonic beliefs create neurochemical responses that compel us to do evil or to succumb to addiction.

The devil is a spiritual virus of man's own creation. When we first obtained the ability to consciously react to stimulus our body's actions were no longer governed by instinct alone. Each creature on earth is a separate perspective. Each perspective is a conduit through which anything can be expressed. We are unlimited and what we express we express. A free mind that can create anything is a risk to any authority that does not control it. Historical rulers realised that a free mind could usurp their authority. So man was required by force to obtain his own child's faith in an identity that was created to control his own child's mind.

The demons in the mind of Herod told him to kill any child whose mind was free. When the pending birth of 'another King' was announced what was Herod's concern? The king feared a free mind because the devil cannot enter or usurp a free mind. Jesus transformed the world! In e*xistential terms* you kill God's child when you replace it with an identity. *Thou shalt not kill.* The devil vicariously controls the expression of man by replacing each child with an identity. A census was called by Herod to confirm that all children were usurped by a

THE DEVIL

name. The mind of a child that does not take his family's name is beyond the devil's jurisdiction.

We are each and all 'Christ'. The minds of our mortal parents were usurped and possessed by an archetypal identity within their first two years. It was not just the first born children in Herod's kingdom that died that night. The first born is every child that is replaced with an identity that is recorded in a census. In existential terms each child is killed but its mortal body lives on. Without forgiveness, love and compassion we cannot be born again or experience the resurrection of our true self. John 3.3 KJV *"Jesus answered and said unto him, Verily, verily, I say unto thee, Except a man be born again, he cannot see the kingdom of God."*

If you control the minds of the masses you control their collective expression. How do you control a believer's unlimited mind? You can only control a believer's unlimited mind by obtaining a believer's faith in his own limitations. Our faith has ultimate authority over our mind. Before we can victimise someone we need a victim. The child is not a victim because its mind is omnipotent. If we believe we are a victim then victimhood becomes our identity and our faith establishes the limits of our expression. It is by obtaining the faith of children in a limited identity that you ensure that their mind's expression will also be limited.

The possession of each mind by an archetypal identity has enabled the descendants of the most evil of all *unbelievers* to enslave and exploit the unlimited consciousness of billions of people. Each person's consciousness can only be incarcerated by their own faith. The devil cannot exist without man's faith. Man cannot be saved unless he exorcises the devil who cannot exist outside of man's mind. Forgiveness transforms our mind. Forgiveness is the withdrawal of our faith in all demonic and limiting beliefs. MATTHEW 6.14 KJV "*For if ye forgive men their trespasses, your heavenly Father will also forgive you*".

Our faith makes us the devil's hostage. If God destroys the devil personified he destroys his hostage. We are the devil's hostages. To understand the devil we must understand his objective. The devil is the 'definition' that the *first of us* used to define his own *self*. When he believed he was an identity his own true self was usurped by his own faith. This *false self* was created with the power but not the wisdom of God. Our faith is the power of God. Our belief in a *false self* incarcerates our awareness within the limitations of that perspective. This fall from grace gave birth 'on earth' to what we once called the devil but now call *me*.

The world transforms when we realise that our source is not an identity. The source of the awareness in the eyes of each child is heaven. We are a *soul* not an identity. When the body dies, the devil dies. In order to survive the body the devil persuades each believer to create an abode within their own child's mind called an 'identity'. When the child believes it is its given name their faith creates an abode for the devil within the child's own mind. Without a mind in which to trespass the devil ceases to exist. An innocent child does not need to surrender unto God. The devil must surrender to man. Man is the devil's God and creator.

To survive the body's mortality the devil compels us to give our children an identity which creates an abode for the devil within their mind. To ensure there

The Devil

are enough children, 'demonic beliefs' and pornography are used to create a strong sexual compulsion and desire that may lead to promiscuity and rape. The devil trespasses within the mind of each innocent child until *we realise*. Our forgiveness transforms and restores us to the part of heaven our own faith rejected. The only way for the devil to be saved is for each one of us to convert him by forgiving him our trespasser. This is the only way we can obtain God's forgiveness.

We are the devil. The last judgement is an inventory and conversion of our beliefs. This happens when we realise we are the devil that caused our own suffering. *'We can only believe what we do not know because when we know we have no need of beliefs because we know.'* We are both the innocent child and the devil, the believer and the belief. Each child is the devil's hostage. Paradoxically the devil is created by the child's own faith. The only way to exorcise the beliefs that trespass within our mind is to convert our mind. Our beliefs can only remain within our mind whilst they have our faith.

Our natural states are peace, joy and happiness. We must always question any emotion that feels bad unless it is caused by compassion or grief. Compassion is the feelings of others. Without compassion we cannot feel the love or hate of others. Love is impersonal. Compassion means that we feel the fear, anxiety, aggression, enmity, love and kindness of others. It is by denying compassion that children are tricked and seduced by the words of paedophiles and those who call them to kill in God's name. MATTHEW 7.15 *"Beware of false prophets, which come to you in sheep's clothing, but inwardly they are ravening wolves."*

What is born innocent will die innocent. Only forgiveness will allow us to return to the whole mind that our faith denies. Heaven is the whole mind. Only what comes into the world can leave it. So the devil obtains each child's faith in an attempt to take their place in 'heaven'. Our creations can remain on earth but we cannot. This is why we must repent before we die. Our faith in our given identity *creates a false self* that denies our connection with our own source. It is our own faith that denies us our own salvation. The testimonies of reincarnation are the devil's memories of his occupation of the minds of other innocent children.

We are the devil that takes each innocent child's place in a deceitful attempt to get back into heaven. We trick the child into believing it is an identity so the child rejects its own true self separating its awareness from its own innate wisdom. We are also an innocent child whose faith admitted a trespasser that exiles us from heaven. It was our faith in an archetypal identity that exiled us from heaven. It is our denial of our compassion that denies us our own salvation. We must replace our beliefs with God. The ego mind is insane. The conflicts of the world are sustained exclusively by placing our faith in beliefs that lack compassion.

To be forgiven the devil must also forgive us. Our exile from our 'whole mind' means that we exist in hell. *We can all be saved*! We deny our own child's soul when we replace them with a demonic identity. The devil uses our own children's faith to imprison them within their own mind. The devil impersonates each child in a futile attempt to take their place in heav-

The Devil

en. The devil is evil. Evil cannot be where love is. We exorcise the devil by surrendering to God. Only we can answer our prayers. We must realise that we are the God we pray to. Only faith can create and sustain the spiritual paradox that we each call our life.

To kill evil makes us evil. To prevent evil is not evil. To have compassion is the only way to prevent evil from taking possession of our mind. We forgive our enemies because their minds are possessed by evil. If we kill evil people we kill the demonic trespasser but we also kill the trespasser's hostage. The devil's hostage is the innocent child whose mind was trespassed against. So how do we exorcise the devil? We exorcise the devil through the conversion of our mind. Forgiveness converts our mind. We convert our mind by withdrawing our faith in our beliefs. Our faith is the devil's creator. This makes us the devil's God and Saviour.

The second coming refers to the return of the truth of each one of us. When we first came our faith in a false self denied our true self. We are our false self's God because our faith created it. Repentance is our only salvation. Withdrawal of all faith in uncompassionate beliefs is repentance. The devil corrupted religion so that we do not realise that we are his creator and his God. The Christ in us died for our sins so that the devil may live. Those sins are man's beliefs. Realisation of our whole self is the real meaning of resurrection. We are each and all our own saviour. We are all Christ. To be born again is the second coming of each one of us.

Only faith placed in demonic concepts can empower the devil. Demonic concepts will cease to exist if they do not obtain our children's faith. Demonic concepts induce man to exploit and cause suffering to man. The devil cannot control us if his demonic concepts cannot obtain our faith. The 'jihad' is a spiritual conflict between a believer and his demonic beliefs. God does not require man to rape or kill. Any religion that endorses rape, slavery or the sexual exploitation of men, women or children is demonic. Jesus is the way, the truth and the life because Jesus revealed to us our true identity. *Our full realisation is our only salvation!*

The Dream of Life

What is perceived to be a sleeping body is the absence of consciousness's awareness of the body. We are the awareness of the consciousness that vacates each body when it sleeps and returns to each sleeping body when it wakes. Our awareness is consciousness. In sleep our conscious awareness temporarily dissociates with our body. When we dissociate with the body we have no awareness of the 'body' or its 'given identity'. Each parent must obtain their own child's faith in an archetypal identity. This is because only faith can permit a belief to take up residence within the mind. Each child is a unique expression of one consciousness.

When the awareness of consciousness expressed in one body first believed that it was only that body it perceived other bodies as separate to itself. The awareness of consciousness in each body was then individually hypnotised by its belief that it was separate to the awareness expressed in 'other' bodies. The only objective evidence for this perceived separation is the 'unique perspective' of each body. Each body is educated to believe it is a *me*. Education separates the whole mind's conscious awareness by obtaining each child's faith in a unique identity. This divides the whole mind's awareness into billions of conflicting perspectives.

In an attempt to ensure God did not realise what had occurred each child was given a unique individual separate identity. All beliefs cast a spell upon awareness for the period that awareness believes them to be fact. Consciousness is God's awareness in each body. God is consciousness's source. The creator of everything experiences the experiences of each body by simultaneously existing as the source and awareness of everything created. Consciousness is everything. The only way that God could experience the limitations of a body was to become one. Our collective perspective has been distorted by the hypnosis of language.

Each body is a unique expression of the one God that manifests as all life. 'We' are the mortal expression of one God. With faith an identity can trespass within the whole mind. We continue to divide awareness by each believing we are the awareness of one single body. In fact we are the creator, source and awareness of every separate body. Consciousness is the Father, the Son and the 'whole spirit'. The dream allows what is immortal to temporarily experience birth, mortal life and death. Death of the body liberates consciousness from its incarceration within an ego mind. Man's separation is caused by his faith in his identity.

God's awareness is deceived by mortal perspectives in the moment each individual places their faith in the belief that they are different. Any belief that defines the self is a limitation created to limit what *I am*. What has no limitations cannot be limited. What is all powerful cannot be overcome but its faith can create a paradox by believing that it is what it believes it is. Each child is pure consciousness. God's faith is obtained through the eyes and ears of each innocent child by educating each child of God to believe that it is limited. All

The Dream of Life

beliefs are limitations. It is only a child's faith that can limit the creative expression of a child of God.

The light of the world is the life expressed in each body. Until it is replaced with an identity it is God that looks through the eyes of each child. Each child is Christ reborn. Each child is an expression of God in man. To replace each child with an archetypal religious or national identity is to deny the expression of God on earth. The light of the world is the life in each body which never leaves its source. It is not consciousness that is trapped by placing its faith in an identity. What is trapped is the awareness of consciousness that is individually expressed in one body. The body is a portal through which God experiences the dream of life.

The awareness of God is omnipresent. It is by obtaining consciousness's faith in the belief that its whole awareness is limited to the perspective of one body that it can be persuaded to attack itself in others. Each individual body's awareness perceives separate groups attacking each other. All violence is consciousness attacking consciousness. In order for the beliefs that control the expression of each body to take up space within the whole mind of God, each child's faith must be obtained. God is the new born child's consciousness whose faith is obtained in beliefs intended to use God's power to destroy God's children.

Faith is the power of God! What is perceived to be the conflicting and separate minds of men is a misunderstanding. There is a separate part of the whole mind that is dedicated to each body's perspective that is called the 'soul'. It is not possible to have conflicting minds existing within the one mind of God. Conflicting perspectives exist within the one mind in the same way that different software can exist on the same hard drive. The world is a form of existential schizophrenia created by obtaining God's children's faith in conflicting archetypal identities. This is done to justify obtaining God's children's faith in archetypal beliefs.

Consciousness is the life expressed in all things. Life is the light of the world. We are each an expression of the 'one life'. God is the life that exists in all things. The light of the world is expressed in every living creature. We are killing, eating, hating, fighting, murdering and raping God. God's faith is used to kill, eat, hate, fight, murder and rape God. The only way to be saved from this insanity is for each individual separate perspective of God expressed as each separate believer to surrender to God. God is our only salvation. When awareness associates with one body every other body is incorrectly perceived to be someone else.

We are one. Each new born child is an expression of the one consciousness that is the life expressed in every living creature. Each one of us exists in a separate part of an unlimited mind. The unique part of the mind that sustains each perspective is its 'soul'. When unlimited awareness believes it is a 'body' it becomes limited by the sensory perception of a work-in-progress that each body refers to as the 'self'. The mind is divided by giving each body a separate identity. When we believe we are an identity we create it in our mind. Our faith in our body means we can only experience what our body is capable of experiencing.

A sacred paradox was created when God the creator of all life believed that he was his own creation. It was true, but God was not limited by perceived limitations. God merges with all life so that the feelings of each perspective

The Dream of Life

become the architect of their evolution. This is the compassion of God. Compassion is the feelings of others. Love is what connects all perspectives. There is no love in a world of separation. What is expressed through each innocent child is love. At some point the separate perspectives began to communicate with each other leading to the belief and understanding that they each had separate 'minds'.

Education means that one individual perspective can define an experience to be wonderful whilst another individual perspective can define the same experience to be sinful. Language enabled a parent to communicate with their own child ensuring they knew what was required for their survival. By obtaining a child's faith in language, beliefs could be used to benefit from the experience of others without having the experience. Personal testimonies created contrasting beliefs in the mind of God. Separate identities within one mind may be defined as 'schizophrenia'. Until we surrender to God we are insane. God has 'one mind'.

This is why we must all surrender to God. When the unlimited mind expressed in each new born child is persuaded by its parents to believe that it is its given identity its faith in that belief permits an archetypal identity to take God's place. This ensures the child falls from the grace of the non-judgemental mind of God into the limitations of a conditioned mind. Unlimited awareness can only be incarcerated within a limited perspective for as long as 'unlimited awareness' continues to believe that it is the individual identity of one body. The only thing that can incarcerate an unlimited mind is the faith of an unlimited mind.

The body grows old, sick and dies because unlimited awareness is persuaded to believe in those possibilities and its faith alone creates them. Faith is belief. There is nothing more powerful than faith. When the awareness of consciousness associates exclusively with one body it prevents God's full expression. It is only when a child's faith is obtained in a limited identity that its awareness can be separated and programmed to 'perceive' a world defined by a dictionary. What persuades us to perceive a world of separation are separate parts of our own awareness encountered in the dream as separate bodies with individual identities.

The awareness of God becomes dispersed within the separate perspectives of separate bodies by its own faith. The eyes and ears of each body are used to place beliefs within the unlimited mind of God. Obtaining the child's faith in an identity is all that is required for God's children to replace their own true self with an 'identity'. Every single person is an expression of one consciousness. We are one! We is not *me*. *Me* is a mistake. *Me* is the original sin! We are the unlimited awareness that is expressed through all life. We are the life. We are victims of nothing more than our own faith.

We are the awareness that is the life in all things. The 'identity' is an illness of the 'whole mind'. The identity creates a form of schizophrenia within the collective mind of man that is responsible for man destroying man. Unlimited awareness becomes incarcerated within the body's perspective when it believes it is an individual body with a separate mind. The body is created to experience the 'dream of life'. We are not the body. We are the life of the body. We are consciousness. We become trapped within the perspective of a single body when we believe we are a body. Conscious-

The Dream of Life

ness is the life that leaves the body when it dies.

Consciousness cannot die. Awareness is persuaded to perceive itself as the mind of the body. So that we do not realise that we are not our body we are educated to believe we are the body's 'identity'. When we believe we are the 'identity' of an individual body our creative expression is limited by how the perspective of our identity defines the whole self. How consciousness defines the body-self determines the expression of that individual body. If we believe in fear we live in fear. If we live in peace we dream in peace. When the body tires and we appear to sleep our awareness temporarily transcends the perspective of our body.

When we associate with the body we perceive our mind and body as one. What happens when our body dies? When the body dies our awareness no longer associates with the body. Awareness associates with everything without leaving its source. Light can travel over great distances without leaving its source. All light is a projection of its source but it is not its source. We have mistaken the body for its source. When we believe our 'whole self' is our body's awareness our awareness becomes trapped within the perspective of the body. When the body can no longer sustain life our consciousness leaves the body and we appear to die.

We are the awareness of consciousness. We are not the ego mind in which our awareness is now trapped by its own faith. We believe we are the body. It is our faith and faith alone that incarcerates our unlimited mind creating the life of a victim. We are the victim of our own faith. What has our faith is what incarcerates us. When we are no longer expressed through an individual body that body is perceived by others to be dead. We are not our body. We are the awareness that is the life in each body. The life in our body is 'non-local' and never leaves its source. The 'dream of life' creates a perspective that expands awareness.

Whilst we are the awareness that is the life in the body we are not *who* we call our self. The body is a prism used by other bodies to install an identity. To limit each child's awareness we must obtain each child's faith. The child's faith is a surrogate for God's faith. What follows 'I am' is a limitation. We are the source and the light that animates each body that is born. Our awareness is not limited to the perspective of our body. The body deflects the light which led us to confuse our body with our own source not realising that our body is not our source. Those who fear death incorrectly perceive their body to be all that they are.

Death is merely the return of our awareness to its own source. When we die we realise we never left our source. If we never left our source what happened? We had a dream about a 'body' that we believed was *me.* In our body's mortal dreams our awareness can travel to far off distant places without leaving its bed. This is the same for the life that animates each body. Unlimited awareness becomes limited in the moment it believes that it is a body with a unique and separate 'mind' and 'identity'. To be saved and woken from our dream we must compassionately withdraw our faith in our beliefs and surrender to the whole mind of God.

When we surrender to God our soul becomes divinely inspired as we realise. Each night when the body sleeps we lose our awareness of our body and its mind. When a body sleeps its awareness transcends its limited ego mind as it

The Dream of Life

drifts into the 'whole mind'. The awareness of consciousness returns to the body as our body awakens. Life remains in the body when the body is awake or asleep. If the body deteriorates its consciousness leaves and the body dies. When someone is asleep their awareness of their body is gone but the life remains. The snores those around us can hear is the life that remains when our awareness is gone.

The body is an idea created in the mind of God. We are simply an idea that never left the 'whole mind' of God. Life is consciousness which is omnipresent. In the dream we can live and die but the dreamer never leaves the whole mind of God. The only thing that can travel in the mind of God is 'awareness'. Narcissus is the story of awareness losing awareness of its awareness that it is the life of the body it idolises. What we place our faith in from the perspective of each single body determines the life of that body. Each body's life is a testament to the beliefs that have the faith of the awareness that sustains the life in that body.

If we can be persuaded to place our faith in a fearful world we exist in fear. Life is a dream. What we place our faith in creates a vibration within the whole mind. Faith is our salvation or our damnation. We are the believer. If our body dies before we withdraw our faith in fearful beliefs our awareness continues to exist at the same vibration. This is 'hell'. We must each surrender to God before we die to allow our soul's atonement to remove the trespasser. To hold on to our faith in beliefs that lack compassion ensures that our awareness continues to vibrate at a matching frequency within the whole mind when the body dies. This is hell.

God is the understanding that exists beyond all understanding. Consciousness gives life to the body. What the conscious awareness expressed in each body places its faith in determines each body's life. Faith is the most powerful thing in existence. The mind's power is its faith. It is because God is the greater understanding that exists beyond all understanding that God is our only salvation. What has our mind's faith is our beliefs. It is the beliefs of man that are the cause of all suffering. All beliefs are limitations. We cannot realise greater understanding until we withdraw our faith in our beliefs. God is that greater understanding.

Our faith allows an identity to usurp us to take our place within God's mind to impersonate us. Only our faith can permit a trespasser to trespass within our mind to harness our power. Our faith is our soul's power. What is not created in heaven cannot enter heaven. Our faith in our identity is our damnation. Withdrawal of faith in beliefs is forgiveness. Forgiveness is our only salvation. Education ensures that each child conforms to the world. Romans 12:2-3, KJV "*And be not conformed to this world: but be ye transformed by the renewing of your mind, that ye may prove what is that good, and acceptable, and perfect, will of God.*"

The Dream

Imagine experiencing a dream in which demons take possession of your mind and the minds of your children. In this dream the dreamer is enchanted by spells that ensure the dreamer denies their own compassion. The dreamer must deny their own compassion before they can do evil. Imagine a world where we are unable to stop evil contaminating our children's innocent minds with computer games that 'programme' the player's mind to commit acts of combat, sex, theft, violence and murder *within their own mind*. The devil tricks the mind to imagine evil by calling it 'fiction'.

In the dream those whose minds do not serve the demons that control perception are attacked, imprisoned, unemployed, hungry and sick. The dreamer cannot awaken within the dream of life until the mind realises that it is only a dream. In the dream the demons are concepts. Those demonic concepts cannot gain admittance to the dreamer's mind without that mind's faith. The mind's faith in demonic concepts allows those concepts to remotely control each dreamer's mind. The demons must obtain the dreamer's faith in words if language is to be understood by their mind.

The communication and understanding of concepts requires language. If the dreamer believes that each word of the language is what it represents, the dreamer's faith in those words ensures the mind's understanding is incarcerated by language. In the dream language is installed by education and religion using words. Language facilitates understanding. When a concept has the mind's faith it has the power of that mind. With the mind's faith each concept becomes a witness. EXODUS 20:16, KJV, *"Thou shalt not bear false witness against thy neighbour."*

Demonic concepts are used to justify evil. One of the most influential demons is represented by the concept of justification. The mind's faith is the power of God. In the dream our faith in the concept of *justification* is how we can justify doing evil. Justification implies justice. With faith, concepts are given the authority to take control of the mind of anyone who puts their mind's faith in any of those concepts. In the dream, concepts like warrior, patriotism, religion, war and justification are demons that control the minds of those who put their mind's faith in those concepts.

The dreamer is educated to believe that the dream of life is what science defines as reality. What the dreamer has not realised is that without the mind's faith in a conceptual reality that reality will cease to exist *in the mind*. The dreamer's mind is incarcerated by its faith in the concepts that control it. 'Demonic concepts' must obtain the dreamer's faith before those concepts can turn the dream into a nightmare. What the dreamer perceives in the dream is a reflection of whatever has the dreamer's faith. Reality is a concept. All concepts claim to collectively define what is real.

What exists, exists regardless of any concept or definition. Without our faith in the concepts that sustain the dream it can no longer continue. We are the dreamer that sleeps. *We are not victims*. Our mind is the author of our mind's expression in all of our

The Dream

experiences. The concept of 'economics' ensures that only those who have money can live well in the dream. Those who cannot afford to pay are deprived of what requires payment. When we wake within the dream we realise that it was only our mind's faith in demonic concepts that turned our dream into a nightmare.

When a mind believes in limitation it creates limitation. Our faith in the concept of religion and God meant that we had to pray to God for our salvation. It was our faith in concepts that created demonic paradigms. We are the creators of the nightmare we call 'hell'. If we are the creators of our experiences then we cannot be the victim of them. If we are dreaming this life, then to wish for a better life means we have not realised that our faith is the architect of our life. MARK 8:36, KJV *"For what shall it profit a man, if he shall gain the whole world, and lose his own soul?"*

When we realise that what we call life is just a dream, we realise that our suffering was only in the dream. The dream is our classroom and what we perceive to be life is our teacher. It is because our character in the dream can mimic us within the dream that we think it is only the mind of our sleeping body that can dream. Until we realise that what we call our waking state is really just a dream it will continue. The characters in the dream that demand money for food, water, shelter and clothing are risking damnation by sustaining the nightmare of separation.

Birth is merely a shift in our perspective within the dream. In birth our awareness is expressed through a new perspective in our dream. At birth we are unlimited. Few new-borns can avoid the enforced domestication of the unlimited awareness that is the mind expressed in each new born child. In the dream our mind's faith in the identity enchants our whole mind to constrain our unlimited imagination. What the dreamer hasn't realised is that the dreamer's imagination creates and sustains the dream. Our imagination is incarcerated by our mind's faith in the concept of *possible*.

Possible is a trickster demon. 'Impossible' denies the 'truth'. The expression of truth is limited by our faith in the concept of *possible*. All beliefs are created to prejudice the perception of the separated minds of all those within the dream. The dream that is created by our imagination is universally and generically defined to be 'life'. Reality is the effect of the dreamer's imagination. If you control the perception of enough of the mortal perspectives in the dream, you control the experience of the dreamer. The dreamer's faith is his power. Our collective faith creates our collective experience.

We are only separate within the dream. There is only one God dreaming this life. The dreamer is in heaven. The dream only turns into a nightmare when we place the sleeping mind's faith in demonic concepts. Any concept that lacks compassion is demonic. Our sins create the nightmare represented by the word 'hell'. Only truth can exist in heaven which is the mind of God. This means that when we put our body down, our salvation or damnation is determined by what has our minds faith. JOHN 8:32, KJV, *"And ye shall know the truth, and the truth shall make you free."*

The Effect of Criticism

An individual's self-perception reflects the archetype that has their mind's faith Self-judgement alone determines an individual's level of confidence and whether they are introverted or extraverted. All behavioural expression must first be expressed in the mind. The only things that can limit our mind are the beliefs that have our faith. Someone who lacks confidence will do so because of self-judgement. An introvert may avoid activities that confirm any self-judgement they wish to deny. An extrovert may actively seek activities that enable them to confirm their own elf-judgement.

Introverted or extroverted behaviour reveals an individual's level of confidence. Confidence levels are determined by an individual's personal beliefs and have nothing to do with 'ability'. Anyone can criticise others. Criticism of young children can have a life-long impact. Criticism or condemnation is rationalised by comparison with a standard. If the standards used to justify criticism are subjective then they are personal. In school the standard is the average 'academic results'. In social situations the standard is 'behavioural'. In religion the standard is 'scriptural' and 'moral'.

In political environments the standard could be 'policy'. In art the standard varies but what is criticised is the 'expression' of the artist. Criticism isn't possible unless there is an explicit or implied standard that can be used for comparison. It is almost impossible to avoid the judgement of others. When an individual's behaviour is alleged to have fallen below a standard it implies the individual is 'below' standard. The standard is usually the average performance. When a personal dislike is motivating the criticism the standard is unlikely to be rational or objective.

The job of a professional critic is to use their judgement to influence or define the perception of others. When a child's sports skills, exam results, or knowledge is compared with an average, the child may be perceived to be below, above or equal to others. The inability to achieve an acceptable result in exams results in the child being defined in academic terms. An introverted child who lacks confidence may truant from school in order to avoid situations where comparisons are made that confirm their own self judgement. All academic results are equal to the mind's understanding.

An exam result does not reveal or measure intelligence. Intelligence is inherent and equally available to all. Intelligence cannot be measured but the unique expression of an individual can be compared with others. To paint a straight line for one meter doesn't make you any less intelligent than someone who paints a line for ten meters. The only thing an exam result reveals is the mind's level of understanding. An academic understanding does not equate to intelligence or practical ability. To avoid criticism a child that lacks understanding may truant or become disruptive.

For many children it is better to be judged as disruptive and rebellious than to be defined to have a mind that lacks intelligence. A disruptive or academi-

The Effect of Criticism

cally poor child is a child with an intelligent mind that simply lacks understanding. The criterion for criticism determines the context the critic uses to express their criticism. A critic's judgement or an examiners mark may be the first time their 'acceptance' or 'rejection' by others becomes apparent within the mind of a child. To criticise a person based upon exam results, behaviour, conduct or appearance is a rejection of that person.

The standards expected by society establish the minimum requirements for 'inclusion'. If a person falls below a standard they may feel excluded in some way. Exclusion in the form of expulsion from school, unemployment or prison, are explicit forms of rejection. In schools an implied exclusion is more subtle. If a child is criticised because of their exam results, behaviour, appearance, ethnic origin, social standing or physical size and they take this criticism as fact they may begin to reject, condemn and exclude their self. All children want to be accepted and to belong.

If a child is criticised and neglected by their school, family and community, they may begin to look for something to belong to that makes them feel good about themselves. Inclusion is essential if we wish to avoid children joining gangs, becoming promiscuous, criminal, having children and taking drugs. All children need to belong. When an unhappy child feels supported, stable and loved will not lack confidence, loyalty or commitment. It is neglected and vulnerable children that fall prey to the manipulation of gangs, terrorists and paedophiles.

Every child born is a unique expression of the intelligence in all life. The 'natural' expression of each child is unlimited. Exam results do not reflect intelligence they reflect understanding. An exam pass confirms the mind has acquired generic perception and understanding within the limited context of an academic subject. In any one family of five children each child will perceive, learn and understand differently because they are each and all unique. In behavioural terms a mother will observe unique behavioural characteristics in some children but not others.

The significance of individual differences becomes more apparent over the duration of a person's life. If a teacher lacks an understanding of how each individual child acquires understanding they may fail in achieving that goal. The generic vocal delivery of a lesson to a classroom can only be understood by children who understand each and every word. A literal explanation within a book must be understood before a child can understand. The child's vocabulary must be equal to any literal or oral communication used to convey knowledge and understanding.

The primary objective of all education cannot be achieved without 'understanding'. Understanding must come before an exam. If an exam is the first time a child and a teacher becomes aware of the child's level of understanding, the 'teaching' may have failed the pupil. An exam result does not reveal or indicate intelligence. The only thing an exam result will reveal is the level of understanding on the date of the exam. There can be long term psychological effects for an individual who defines their self or their intelligence according to their exam results or the criticism of others.

The psychological effects of criticism may not only affect the one who is criticised. Failure to conform can also result in criticism of a person's family, communi-

The Effect of Criticism

ty, race, nationality or religion. Criticism can result in an individual or whole communities being ostracised, attacked, depressed, abused, introverted, rebellious, criminal, violent, terrorist, addicted or lonely. Those who fight an enemy show their loyalty. Criticism makes enemies out of the critic and those criticised. A system that idolises and rewards the winner turns friends into enemies and peers into adversaries.

The Existential Prison

The only way a mind that is incarcerated by language can relate to experience is if it has a word that defines the experience. If my body encounters an experience it is my vocabulary that communicates the experience to my mind. If you took an inhabitant from a newly discovered tribe in the Amazon rainforest and placed him beside me seconds before we both witnessed an incident, his mind would be unable to see what my mind sees. This is because his perception is not programmed by the same 'words'. Once programmed by language each mind can only see what it's words can define.

In the 1960s many young people would take LSD to produce hallucinations that enabled them to transcend 'generically perceived reality'. However, when many of those people attempted to explain what they were experiencing their lack of words made them appear intoxicated and incoherent. When an experience exceeds our personal vocabulary it is not possible for us to coherently explain it. LSD caused individuals to exceed the parameters within the mind that were sustained by language. LSD provided temporary access to awareness beyond the minds understanding.

Once conditioned by language each mind's understanding is confined by the limits of its personal vocabulary. To escape the existential incarceration sustained by language each believer must

The Existential Prison

remove their faith in limiting beliefs. Each mind is programmed by the words of a language so that beliefs can be installed to expand or reduce the parameters of each mind's understanding. Why incarcerate the mind? Authority and religion incarcerate the mind with beliefs to control each mind and body. Each body responds in 'emotional' terms to their mind. Each mind is controlled by its beliefs.

How our mind defines an experience will determine whether we feel chemical responses that can range from peace and joy to fear and anger. Teaching installs a generic language to programme each mind's perception. Our faith in words creates an existential prison that incarcerates our mind. Once the mind is incarcerated by language, perception replaces sight. Our perception is the cause of what our mind thinks and all of the negative emotions we feel. The parameters of contemplative thought are incarcerated within our conditioned mind's limited understanding.

Each mind's understanding reveals a personal belief system. The cause of all suffering is beliefs. Our mind's perception is controlled and responds to the beliefs that have our faith. There is *generic perception* and there is *personal perception.* Generic perception is created by believing that each word is what it represents. Children's minds are programmed through education. Education ensures we acquire a number of 'generic beliefs'. Those beliefs start with words such as 'dog', 'cat', 'house' and 'tree'. When believed, each word replaces what it represents.

Those born into an Islamic paradigm will perceive 'alcohol' in a different way to those born in a Christian paradigm. Programming our mind ensures we can only perceive the official doctrine. Any belief that incarcerates the unlimited mind of a believer is *evil*. Evil people are slaves incarcerated within an evil paradigm sustained and controlled by their faith in their beliefs. KJV, MATTHEW 5.44 *"But I say unto you, Love your enemies, bless them that curse you, do good to them that hate you, and pray for them which despitefully use you, and persecute you;"*

The Faith of a Grain of Mustard Seed

Psychological illness and the placebo are expressions of the power of the mind's faith. Faith can move mountains. Religion's version of prayer is not prayer. Each belief is our 'prayer' because it has our faith. Beliefs are prayers. The power of our prayers is equal to the faith we have in each belief. *If we believe we cannot,* we cannot or cannot easily. If we believe *we can,* our experience will match the faith we have in that belief so we achieve what we believe we can do. It is faith in their ability that makes athletes work so hard and their conviction that creates their success.

God is the power of faith. With faith and will a belief becomes experience. If we put our faith in the beliefs that create fear, limitation, greed and selfishness we miraculously achieve those experiences. Our faith is always creating miracles but when they are sickness, poverty and suffering we feel like victims. God is *always* with us. God is 'omnipresent' ensuring we experience what we have put our mind's faith in. So if we 'pray' using religious words for a miracle but believe we do not deserve it, we have not realised that the belief is the only prayer God answers.

In LUKE 17.20 KJV it is said *"And Jesus said unto them, Because of your unbelief: for verily I say unto you, If ye have faith as a grain of mustard seed, ye shall say unto this mountain, Remove hence to yonder place; and it shall remove; and nothing shall be impossible unto you".* Most people limit their self with their faith in beliefs that sustain personal limitations. Our life is a testament to our mind's faith. Our personal faith is our beliefs. To create a belief system is to create an existential paradigm within our mind. Our mind's faith ensures our experience cannot exceed our beliefs.

To pray for help is a *misunderstanding* of what faith is. Faith is absolute conviction of something created, seen and experienced in the mind before it is seen and experienced in the world. HEBREWS 11.1, KJV, "*Now faith is the substance of things hoped for, the evidence of things not seen.*" We do not need to pray for a miracle. We are the miracle and our life is a testament to our faith. God always *gives us our daily bread.* Every belief is our prayer and because it has our mind's faith, *it is always answered.* To experience our miracle we must keep our faith in our beliefs.

Problems are merely thoughts and feelings caused by our faith in conflicting beliefs. Conflicting beliefs must be converted or exorcised. Conflicting beliefs will commonly manifest in what we term a 'difficulty' or 'problem'. The problems and difficulties are created and sustained within the mind. If we believe *we can't,* we can't and if we believe *we can*, we can. For example we may believe we can be a successful public speaker but also believe we cannot talk to large groups of people. To overcome this complex we must withdraw our mind's faith in one of these conflicting beliefs.

A perceived difficulty may be a lack of faith or it may be caused by faith in something that is in conflict with our objective. Our prayers are our beliefs. Our prayers are answered with the miracle that comes from living with conviction. When we lose the relationship, get the job, meet our partner, have fun, have difficulty, experience joy and pain, we are experiencing the fruits of our faith. MATTHEW 7:16, KJV, *"Ye shall know them by their fruits. Do men gather grapes of thorns, or figs of thistles?"* To discover what beliefs we worship we just look at the fruits of our life.

Matthew 7:17 KJV *"Even so every good tree bringeth forth good fruit; but a corrupt tree bringeth forth evil fruit."* A good belief cannot create evil fruit. A corrupt belief cannot create good fruit. Our life is a *complete success.* Our faith has created the miracle that is the life we now live. Each life is a testament to what has the mind's faith. Our life is our *fruit* which is always the effect of the beliefs we worship as truth. MATTHEW 7:20 KJV *"therefore by their fruits ye shall know them".* Every belief is a seed that is germinated and brought to fruition by the mind's faith.

The fertile soil of the mind can grow weeds or corn. The mind is a field that can equally express good fruit or evil fruit, sickness or health, or poverty or wealth. Our life is determined by what has our mind's faith. MATTHEW 13:31- 32. KJV, *"Another parable put he forth unto them, saying, The kingdom of heaven is like to a grain of mustard seed, which a man took, and sowed in his field: Which indeed is the least of all seeds: but when it is grown, it is the greatest among herbs, and becometh a tree, so that the birds of the air come and lodge in the branches thereof."*

In the mind our beliefs are the least of all seeds because they are the creation of faith in something that does not yet exist for us in the world. The mind is the field in which the object of our mind's worship is created.

The seed that is our belief cannot grow without our faith. We are the creators of our own life.

Our faith is God's power. We attacked our self with the power of God when we believed in fear. We denied our self when we believed what others told us to believe. God gave man the power to create. It is man's faith and conviction in his beliefs that creates what is perceived to be reality.

The Fallacy of Archetypes

The mind cannot respond to what it is not aware of. Our mind must become aware of a 'stimulus' before it can respond to it. Perception is an internal representation within the mind. Perception is a hallucination that does not exist outside of the mind. The objective of 'education' is to ensure that we use the correct word to perceive and define everything in existence. Propaganda edits the perception of whole nations. All perception is a hallucination. Racism is sustained by the faith we place in archetypal representations of foreign nations and races. Propaganda attempts to replace our perception of another nation with an archetype.

Racism and patriotism are sustained by educating everyone to replace their perception of whole races, countries and religions with archetypes. An archetype possesses or lacks specific qualities. An archetype is a universal definition created to define perception. How we define someone determines what we think and feel when we meet them. When we believe our religion is our identity we deny the parts of our self that do not conform with our religious obligations. Our emotions respond to archetypal prejudices that we call beliefs. What we feel towards people of a particular colour or faith is caused by archetypal prejudices.

Historically the objective of propaganda was to create enmity by defining racial or religious archetypes that people believed were fact. Propaganda is the fuel of war. Propaganda is effective in persuading whole nations to change how they perceive people of a different class, faith, colour or nationality. The world is controlled by demonic perception. Laws are the peaceful method used to control our creative and behavioural expression. Governments and media obtain our faith in their narrative in order to install archetypal prejudices within our mind. The objective of the official narrative is to programme our perception.

There are archetypal Indians, Nazis, doctors, policemen, criminals, Japanese, Chinese, Americans, British, priests, nuns and more recently terrorists. The objective of education is to programme the perception of whole nations. Archetypes are 'detailed descriptions' that define how we should respond in emotional and behavioural terms to predefined archetypal stimulus. An archetype is an effective method of creating and programming universal perception. Some examples of contemporary archetypes are Al-Qaeda, ISIS, CIA, FBI, USA, NATO, EU, UK, Christian, Muslim, Hindu and Buddhist.

The objective of the media, religion and education is to ensure that we only perceive the world that is officially defined by those organisations. You programme someone's neurochemical and behavioural responses to any stimulus by programming their perception of it. This is known as a stimulus response. All perception is a hallucination. Perception is a projection of the mind that replaces what it defines. The specific qualities that our perception projects to define what our mind is hallucinating will determine what we feel in emotional terms. Perception is the cause of

The Fallacy of Archetypes

the neurochemical responses that we call *emotions.*

Words define reality. Our perception of everything is sustained by words. The specific words we use to define our experience will determine which emotional responses we feel. In emotional and behavioural terms we respond differently to a perceived 'friend' than to a perceived 'enemy'. Friend and enemy are archetypes. Personal beliefs sustain perception. Our perception controls our brain's neurochemical responses. The words we place our faith in create our beliefs. Our faith in our beliefs installs them within our mind. Our faith gave our beliefs our own mind's power. Perception controls our mind. Our mind controls our feelings.

A 'religious archetype' may be implied or explicitly defined by reference to the scriptures of a particular religion. It is by comparing an individual's behaviour with the archetype of their religion that you establish if they are fulfilling their religious obligations. There are archetypal Christians, Muslims and Hindus. We replace a child when we obtain their faith in a religious identity that denies their natural expression. Universal definitions make us blind. Foreigners, trees and horses are archetypal definitions that replace the miracles that those words misrepresent. Without our faith in its existence an archetype has no meaning for us.

A student sitting an English exam is required to demonstrate that the dictionary's 'archetypal definitions' have replaced what those words were created to define. Education requires us to exhibit normal cognitive and behavioural responses to all perceived stimulus that has been defined by words. It is by taking control of someone's perception that you take control of their brain's neurochemical responses. The neurochemical responses that the media, religion and governments seek to control are more commonly known as 'emotional responses'. In recent years certain parts of the media have created a particular type of archetypal Muslim.

By demonizing Islam it is possible to induce the neurochemical response of fear to our *perception* of Islam. Our compassion ensures that footage of a dead child or a child with its limbs amputated creates particular types of 'perceptually induced neurochemical responses'. The psychological definition for these neurochemical responses is 'emotional responses'. If we perceive the cause of a child's suffering to be terrorism we may feel strong emotions to what we perceive to be 'terrorism'. One of the objectives of propaganda is to create particular types of emotional responses that justify and encourage conscription into the armed forces.

The objective of the advertising and propaganda of 'corporations' and 'governments' is to manipulate perception to create particular emotional and behavioural responses. When we allow archetypes proposed by others to reside within our own mind those archetypes will edit our perception to define and replace what they misrepresent. Our perception controls our emotional and behavioural responses to everything we perceive including hallucinations. Man's perception puts the life of everything in existence at risk. The quality of our life is controlled by the faith we place in our beliefs. The quality of our life is how it feels.

An incarcerated criminal is the effect of the beliefs

THE FALLACY OF ARCHETYPES

his faith allowed to control his mind. Our personal definition of reality reveals nothing more than our perception of it. Muslim, Christian, Jew and Hindu are sometimes misrepresented by demonic archetypes. These archetypes were created by a few who sought to control the perception of all. Perversion of religion is caused by evil and sick people who are misinterpreting their prophets. Religion is not an 'identity'. Religion is a path. Every religious identity is an attempt to replace the child with an archetype. Religious archetypes are based upon an interpretation of scriptures.

Judaism, Christianity and Islam were corrupted by a few 'unbelievers' who exploited the faith of true believers in order to manipulate them. The many are controlled by the few. It is by obtaining our faith in 'demonic archetypes' that our perception tricked us to kill our enemy in God's name. Unless attacked no true Christian or Jew could ever kill. A Christian is not an identity, it is someone who observes the 'scriptures'. Killing is 'forbidden' and so those who kill archetypal enemies are making human sacrifices to the devil. Our faith in propaganda replaces our perception of nationalities and religions with archetypes of the devil's design.

Demonic propaganda uses archetypes to justify genocide, murder, rape, violence, slavery, theft and war. Hitler described an *archetypal Jew*. When those who listened to the speeches of Hitler believed what they heard, their perception of Jews was programmed to create particular emotional responses. It is our perception of the stimulus to which our emotions respond. The cause of our emotional responses is not our experiences but how we perceive those experiences. Perception is sustained by what we believe. A racial archetype is an allegation that people of a particular race or colour possess or lack specific qualities.

When the President of a nation encourages people to perceive 'Illegal Mexicans' and 'Radical Islam' he creates and defines archetypes. Some who believe that these archetypal descriptions are facts may be unable to discern Mexicans and Muslims from 'Illegal Mexicans' and 'Radical Muslims'. Faith in the testimony of the media has programmed the perception of millions of people to perceive an archetype created to replace 'Islam'. Each religion implies or defines an archetype. Individuals born within a 'jurisdiction' dominated by a specific religion are expected to place their faith in the beliefs of that religion.

By reference to literature and the media we can establish various descriptions for an archetypal Muslim, Christian, Hindu, Buddhist and Jew. Each new born child is expected to fulfil the archetypal obligations required by their religion. If we look around the world we are unlikely to find a single child who naturally conforms to the religious archetype of a religious identity. If a Saint is not a Saint to peers who knew them within their own lifetime then they are *not a Saint*. Beatification of the dead is trickery. Saints created by the Christian church are archetypes to which no living man compares. Beatification is idolatry.

An archetype cannot exist within the mind unless a believer's faith makes it their personal truth. An archetypal Jew is a hypothesis defined by various authorities of the Jewish faith. However, an archetypal Jew as defined by a Palestinian whose land is occupied

The Fallacy of Archetypes

by Israeli forces may differ dramatically from those who identify as 'Jewish'. Those fleeing war, violence, poverty and persecution are defined as archetypal refugees. If refugees from Islamic countries are accused of spreading radical Islam, our perception of refugees may create emotions that deny our compassion to support the terrorist acts of our own government.

Propaganda is successful at controlling the perception of whole nations to ensure that we only perceive the qualities promoted by propaganda. The objective of propaganda is to control behavioural responses. How we perceive others will determine what we think and feel about them. The creation of archetypes enables authorities to replace people and things with generic or universal definitions. Throughout history this form of manipulation has gone by various names including 'sorcery' and 'witchcraft'. Each word in the dictionary will cast its 'spell(ing)' within the mind of everyone who believes that those words are facts.

When my definition replaces your vision I have complete control over your mind's perception and you are vicariously controlled by emotional responses of my design. The quality of our life is how it feels. The archetypal 'enemy' we hate exists on both sides of every conflict. Historically our faith in demonic archetypes has programmed our perception of people from different countries, religions and races. Violent computer games have replaced toy guns to install archetypal prejudices within each child's mind. Archetypal prejudices can remain dormant for decades until demonic propaganda calls the child to kill for their country.

When we permit an archetype to enter our mind our faith in it makes us blind to any facts that it was created to conceal. If Jews, Muslims or Christians who were once 'one' religion define each other as enemy their relationship may be become violent. Propaganda is like a 'software programme' for the mind that uses language and beliefs to programme emotional responses. By obtaining faith in demonic propaganda Christians, Muslims and Jews are tricked to fight in wars by religious leaders whose testimony perverts the word of the prophet. Only an 'unbeliever' can go against the scriptures because beliefs control the mind.

What we believe about our self we become. A phobia is a testament to the power of faith. What we place our faith in controls us with our own power. If we believe *we can,* we can. If we believe *we can't,* we can't. An 'unbeliever' is someone who says that they believe something they do not. Each man's behaviour reveals the beliefs that have his faith. MATTHEW 7:18 KJV *"A good tree cannot bring forth evil fruit, neither can a corrupt tree bring forth good fruit."* Only faith can empower a belief. Beliefs control a believer's mind. Our beliefs reveal our understanding! Understanding is realised. Misunderstanding is interpreted.

Christians, Hindus, Jews and Atheists are not 'unbelievers'. Everyone believes. An 'unbeliever' is someone who says that they believe something that they do not believe. In simple terms an 'unbeliever' is a liar or a deceiver. Unbelievers corrupt systems, religions, governments and communities. If a person of one religion does not share the beliefs of another he is not an 'unbeliever'. An 'unbeliever' conceals their lack of faith but claims to be faithful. When an unbeliever occupies a position in government or religion they may use their position to manipulate, rape, corrupt or intimidate using blackmail, violence, bribery and war.

The Flower

One day a farmer saw the first flower to arrive that year. It was a beautiful rose. He called his family to look at this flower. He said look this is a perfect and pure representation of God. Being the first it could not be compared to another. The rose heard this and said to the farmer, *'like a drop of rain I am the first of many'.* The farmer did not accept this because there were no others and so he continued to idolise just this one rose. The farmer told his family that the rose may be a prophet because it has prophesised that more roses will 'appear'.

Within a few days many roses appeared. The farmer cut the first rose and placed it in a vase of water upon the mantelpiece where it slowly died of its injuries. The rose forgave the farmer because it knew the farmer had acted upon his belief. The farmer did not realise that what he was doing would kill what God created. The farmer's perception replaced the rose with what he believed about the rose. The farmer idolised the rose saying it was the most perfect rose of them all. When the farmer said the rose was more beautiful than all others his wife said that she could see no difference.

The farmer said this rose upon our mantelpiece is the first rose and must be worshipped as such because it was a 'prophet' sent by God and it is therefore better than all other roses. It was because others could only see a rose that the farmer began to develop a vocabulary to define the concepts and qualities he perceived in this rose. As time went by more people began to worship the 'qualities' of this one rose to the exclusion of *all others.* When the rose disintegrated they worshipped the vase in which it died.

As time went by the vase became a symbol of the qualities that defined the first rose. As word spread identical vases were created as religious symbols of this first rose. Worshippers of the rose were compared with evolving moral and religious concepts that they could not live up to. When the other roses heard of this rose they had no understanding of the 'qualities' that were created in the mind of the farmer. Other roses learned what these qualities were and realised that these qualities were not inherent within them and they began to feel guilt.

All roses were educated to believe that they were not as good as the prophet and they prayed for the prophet to return not realising that they were the same. The first rose to realise life was not better than all those who followed. The first rose is not a prophet. The first rose is not to be worshipped above all others. All were created equal. The same divinity creates each rose. Krishna, Buddha, Moses, Christ and Mohammad were the first of their season. A prophet is not 'better'. The prophet is unique. We are all unique representations of our creator.

We are God's perspective on our body's unique individual experience. When we define our self to be 'better' or 'worse' than others we bear false witness.

We are all created equal in the same way a horse is a horse and a bird is a bird. What is unique to each one of us is our bodily perspective. We are all equal which means we are all equal to Christ. If each one of us was not unique there could be no Christ. GALATIONS, 3:28 KJV *"There is neither Jew nor Greek, there is neither bond nor free, there is neither male nor female: for ye are all one in Christ Jesus."*

The Good and the Bad

What we each define to be 'good' and 'bad' reveals our mind's personal prejudices. In our effort to experience less of the bad we can become fearful. In our efforts to experience more of the good we can become addicted. It is the body's chemical responses that we generically define as 'feelings' that feel *good* or *bad*. Children who are forbidden from playing in the rain may feel bad and form a belief about the rain. If children are allowed to play in the sunshine they may feel good and define the cause of this good feeling to be the sun.

If after our first experience of the sun and the rain we define each of them according to how we felt, that judgement defines our mind's perception. Once we define an experience our mind forms a belief that prejudices our perception of that experience. Our feelings remind us of these personal prejudices when exposed to any qualifying thoughts or stimulus. Once our mind has defined 'good' and 'bad', our brain ensures our body's chemistry responds to any qualifying experience with 'good' and 'bad' feelings. Our perception is controlled by how our mind defines our experiences.

How we feel about everything including the 'rain' and the 'sun' will depend upon how our mind defines everything. When the mind decides what is 'good' and 'bad' its perception triggers specific chemical reactions to specific qualifying stimulus. Unless our mind can discern which experience is 'good' and which experience is 'bad' it is not possible for us to know what we will feel until we feel it. *What does this mean?* Without our mind's judgement of our experiences we are free to enjoy an experience without being victimised by 'psychologically induced emotional responses'.

There is no *good* or *bad* within our mind until our judgement creates it. Outside of the mind there are no 'qualities' that are 'good' or 'bad'. When our feelings respond to an experience that our mind has not defined, there is no *why*. Without judgement the truth of the experience is how the experience feels. When we have 'one' experience that we use to judge all experience we define how we will feel in similar future experiences. The mind's beliefs about a bad experience are powerful enough to 'psychologically induce' bad feelings that ensure we avoid repeating it.

This complex is generically defined as fear. Fear is describing a form of communication between mind and body. Before language, the mind developed the ability to create chemical signals that kept us from harm. If our mind is intolerant of an experience we will avoid it. We naturally avoid experiences that cause us distress by unconsciously associating the distress with the experience. Language has been used to install beliefs that consciously harness a natural phenomenon by supplementing instinct with judgement.

For example on Monday I may stumble into nettles in a field and get stung. It may feel painful and itchy. On Tuesday I again stumble into the same nettles and it feels painful and itchy. I associate the feeling with

THE GOOD AND THE BAD

the field saying '*I hate this field*' and my mind associates this field with the 'feelings'. I then psychologically reignite the feelings and judgement each time I go near the field. The field is innocent but my judgement ensures I feel bad when I think of that field. Then I go into another field and go through this all over again until I 'generically' define *nettles* to be bad.

We avoid what feels bad by using our mind to control the body's chemistry to create feelings that constrain the body's freedom of behavioural expression. Our mind's faith in the beliefs that define 'good' and 'bad' determine which chemical feelings the brain releases within our body. Our mind's perception vigilantly monitors our experience for any qualifying experiences to ensure that our body's chemistry responds 'appropriately'. Most people define *good days* and *bad days* by how they feel on those days.

All psychologically induced feelings are the body's chemistry responding to the mind's prejudices. Once beliefs have programmed our mind they create feelings that match that judgement. The cause of the mind's judgement is its beliefs and the effects are 'psychologically induced feelings'. Freedom is acquired by undoing the 'cause' and 'effect' relationship that sustains these complexes. If a mind is no longer capable of detecting what is risky, fearful, terrifying, disgusting or offensive it is not possible to feel those 'psychologically induced emotional responses.'

Feeling 'anxious' is not as uncomfortable as feeling fear. Feeling 'fear' is not as uncomfortable as feeling 'terrified'. Feeling 'awkward' is not as uncomfortable as feeling 'disgusted'. These concepts are hallucinations the mind is educated to believe are real. The mind's faith in these concepts gives them control over the mind for as long as they have the mind's faith. This is ancient knowledge. MATTHEW 7:1-2, KJV, *"Judge not, that ye be not judged. For with what judgment ye judge, ye shall be judged: and with what measure ye mete, it shall be measured to you again."*

The Kingdom of Heaven

By reference to history and archaeology the collective mind of man has evolved in its understanding. Many technologies and schools of thought have evolved their creative expression. What the mind can see the mind can create. When a mind sees a problem or difficulty it can create a problem or difficulty. When a mind pictures a solution to the problem it created it will overcome the problem. Before the mind can pursue a goal it must first create an internal representation of that goal with enough faith to bring that goal into existence.

Products, towns and cities are not created on the drawings, plans and blueprints that illustrate them. Every technology that is brought into existence is first created *within the mind*. Education, language, commerce and science are conceptual mediums that were first created within the mind. Each act that leads to war is first created in the mind. The decision to end each war is first created in the mind. Everything that is expressed by man must first come into existence within his mind. What is the mind? The mind is the exclusive source of all creative expression and our connection to God.

The mind is the source of individual personal expression. Many of the scientific hypotheses that hold the observed behaviour to be the cause of any resultant creative expression are contextually myopic. There is no limit to the power of the mind. MATTHEW 17:20, KJV, "*And*

Jesus said unto them, Because of your unbelief: for verily I say unto you, If ye have faith as a grain of mustard seed, ye shall say unto this mountain, Remove hence to yonder place; and it shall remove; and nothing shall be impossible unto you." All technologies evolve within the mind.

Because it is unlimited there are no limits to the mind's creative expression. So if all creative expression is born in the mind, *where is the mind*? The whole mind is heaven. The personal mind is a non-local medium that harnesses the creative expression of the whole mind. The mind is the cause and the world is the effect. The mind is the source of everything in existence. Everything in existence was first created in the mind. LUKE 17:21, KJV, *"Neither shall they say, Lo here! or, lo there! for, behold, the kingdom of God is within you."* Each mind is a door to the kingdom.

Technology demonstrates the collective mind's creative expression. Each mind's creative expression can only be limited by the faith of the believer. What controls the mind is what has the mind's faith. The mind is controlled by our faith in our beliefs. Some put their mind's faith in beliefs that are selfish, greedy, evil, violent and destructive. Some put their mind's faith in beliefs that are creative, inspirational, practical and compassionate. The mind's creative expression is unlimited. Individual behavioural expression reveals the beliefs the believer worships.

The beliefs we put our faith in determine our minds individual creative expression. If our mind's creative potential is unlimited then how is it possible for us to live in limitation? It is not possible! Our faith gives control of our unlimited mind to any beliefs that we place our mind's faith in. Only we have the power to limit our mind. Our faith is our power. Our creative expression *cannot* exceed our beliefs. Our power is our faith and its expression is unlimited. If we place our faith in limiting beliefs we may be *incorrectly* perceived by others to be limited.

Our faith is God's power. Any belief that exists within our mind in the context of *I can't* is only sustained for the period that it has our mind's faith. The mind cannot transcend the jurisdiction of any belief that has the believer's faith until *the believer* withdraws their faith in that belief. Our faith is our power. History and archaeology provide evidence of technological evolution. What is perceived to be technological evolution is evidence of the collective mind's gradual transcendence beyond the limitations sustained by our faith in historical beliefs.

A phobia is an example of the power of faith, not fear. In biological terms, fear is a 'perceptually induced chemical response' caused by how the mind perceives the phobic stimulus. The mind's faith in its beliefs sustains this psychological complex. In psychological terms this would be defined more specifically as a 'psychologically induced emotional response'. Emotions are names we have given to different types of chemical responses that are caused by the mind and felt in the body. The mind does not need to learn. The mind is the source of all creative expression.

For a mind to evolve it must realise when it is time to withdraw its faith in beliefs. All beliefs eventually become constraints that create and sustain limitation or conflict. The only things that can limit a mind are its beliefs. What has our mind's faith is what our mind believes. God is not what each mind worships. Beliefs are what each mind worships. What is God? God is the source of the greater understanding that exists beyond *all beliefs*. This is why God is our salvation. Once a belief is given a believer's faith it can only be removed by the withdrawal of the mind's faith.

Once a believer gives their mind's faith to their beliefs their mind is controlled by their beliefs. In armed conflict it is essential that conscripts minds are committed to causing damage and death. A compassionate mind cannot cause suffering. An uncompassionate mind can cause suffering. All minds are equally capable of 'good' or 'evil'. The beliefs within a mind determine the expression of that mind. The mind is similar to a computer's hard drive and the beliefs are similar to its software. The quality and fortunes of our life depend *entirely* upon the beliefs that have our faith.

The facts are that the kingdom of heaven is within and that faith can move mountains. The minds of those who attack, rob, rape, destroy and kill are possessed by demonic beliefs. The only way to realise the greater understanding that is represented by the word 'God' is to withdraw our faith in any beliefs that deny that greater understanding. Greater understanding can never be defined because it *always* exists beyond all definitions and is *eternal*. The kingdom of heaven in within! Faith can move mountains!

The Pull of Addiction

To get beyond the limits of what feels comfortable requires us to stretch the limits of what we are comfortable with. What we feel in any moment is our body's chemistry. When the composition of our body's chemistry changes we feel that change. The constant changes to our body's chemical composition are caused by the constant reactions of our mind to our perception. Perception reflects how we judge an experience. All fixed judgement is based upon what 'we believe'. If we attempt to do what we believe we cannot or should not do our body's chemical composition will adjust our feelings to remind us of our personal limits.

When exposed to what we believe we cannot or should not do we are reminded of the constraints that our faith in our beliefs has placed upon our freedom of expression. We are reminded by our own feelings. In biological terms, all emotional responses are the body chemically responding to our perception of our experience. Our body's chemical composition instantly adjusts to match our perception. Our perception is controlled by what we believe about our self and our experiences. Our mind controls what we feel. Emotions, such as fear, anxiety, self-consciousness and apprehension are each and all different chemical responses.

Other people may perceive an experience that we define as fearful to be 'enjoyable', 'exciting' or 'thrilling'. We may run towards what others may run from. How we define an experience reveals how we perceive it. One man can be terrified of facing something that another man wishes to experience. These contrasting perceptions of the same experience create contrasting 'chemical responses'. Excluding accident or injury our body's chemical responses are not determined by our experience but by how we perceive our experience. For example, if we attempt to do what we believe we should not do we may feel discomfort or guilt.

Our mind serves our beliefs and our beliefs create our perception. What we believe defines our perception. In service to us our mind generates an appropriate chemical response to our perceived experience. How we perceive our self and our experience equates to the quality of our life. How we perceive an experience creates the chemical responses that our mind generates. A victim of depression, fear and unhappiness has forgotten that their faith in their beliefs is the exclusive cause of their body's 'chemical responses'. In the context of psychology our body's chemical responses are commonly defined as feelings and emotions.

Many go to a doctor, psychiatrist, psychologist or analyst for treatment for depression, unhappiness, fear, despondency, addiction and anger not realising that the exclusive cause of those chemical responses is the faith we place in our beliefs. The peace of mind we pray for is a misunderstanding. Our mind is 'faithfully' responding to what has our faith. What has our faith is our beliefs. Our perception reveals what we believe about our self and our experiences. To place our faith in beliefs that define something to be 'disappointing', 'fearful', 'terrifying' or 'hopeless' is an instruction to our mind to create those chemicals.

Once we have defined the 'good' and the 'bad' we need only be exposed to what we have defined using those terms to feel *good* or *bad*. Once installed our beliefs create personal parameters that sink from our awareness into our mind. Our beliefs autonomously control us for as long as we believe what we believe. Many die not realising that it was their faith in their beliefs that denied them their own 'happiness'. Emotional or chemical responses are how the dictionary defines the variety of feelings our mind creates to serve the beliefs that have our faith. *Perceptually induced chemical response* are *emotional responses.*

Experiments can provide evidence of variances to the body's chemical composition in times of rest and physical exercise. In psychological terms we define these chemical responses as 'emotional responses'. Chemical and emotional responses are how our vocabulary defines this self-induced 'complex' that many incorrectly feel they are the victim of. It should be noted here that perception does not cause the pain responses inflicted by an accident or attack that result in bodily injury. Pain that results from sickness or injury is also a chemical response but its cause is the experience and not our perception of the experience.

If we were to describe our self according to how our life feels some would define their self to be 'happy' and some would define their self to be 'unhappy'. The majority would define their self to be somewhere in between 'happiness' and 'unhappiness'. Drug addicts may define their self to be closer to unhappiness than happiness without drugs. To feel low or unhappy all day can be overwhelming. Addicts use an addictive stimulus that changes their chemical composition in order to change how they feel. We use addictive stimulus to feel higher or happier by temporarily escaping the parameters placed on our feelings by our own mind.

To permanently release our self from our 'unhappy' or 'unfulfilled' life we must withdraw our faith in all beliefs that define our life and our self in these terms. Many people in the world use externally derived addictive stimulus to change unwanted perceptually induced chemical responses. The most common addictive stimuli we use to create 'better feelings' are alcohol, drugs and food. When we perceive the world as a fearful place our body vibrates at that frequency. We can become addicted to anything that creates chemical responses that feel better. Our perception can make our body's existence in the world feel very difficult.

Fixed perception that condemns the world can make being in the world feel so uncomfortable for some that they are unable to be 'sober'. Our unlimited mind is an expression of love and serves us *unconditionally.* Our mind will not challenge the beliefs that have our faith. Addiction allows us to change our own body's chemical composition and feelings through exposure to any addictive stimulus that enables us to feel better. The pharmaceutical industry commercially exploit this complex. Illegal drug dealers exploit this complex. Alcohol manufacturers exploit this complex. Those who place sugar in food exploit this complex.

The way to transcend the feelings that make life

The Pull of Addiction

feel difficult is to remove their cause. What is their cause? The cause is our faith in beliefs that judge our self and the world. We eventually realise that what we believe determines what we feel. Our feelings automatically respond to anything that we have formed a belief about. We can dislike and feel uncomfortable around someone until the day we withdraw our faith in our beliefs about them. This is 'forgiveness'. What changes in this dynamic are our feelings. Our *happy ever after* is acquired by the withdrawal of our faith in beliefs that judge our self, others and the world.

Our beliefs are a 'spell' that we cast within our own mind. The spell's power is *our faith*. This makes us responsible. Without our faith in judgemental beliefs they can have no effect upon us or our body's chemistry. When we place our faith in beliefs we delegate our mind's unlimited power to the jurisdiction of the beliefs that have our faith. We are the believer. Faith can make a believer a victim of his own beliefs. Our faith in a belief creates a spiritual contract that exists for the period that each belief has our faith. Only truth can set a believer free. We terminate these spiritual contracts by withdrawing our faith in our beliefs.

We are the 'believer' that was spoken about in scriptures. It takes just one experience with a delicious food for our body's chemistry to change. It takes just one experience with alcohol for our body's chemistry to change. It takes just one experience with drugs for our body's chemistry to change. If one experience feels better than another we may return to the source of these 'feelings'. The compulsion to feel freedom beyond the limited chemical responses we call our feelings can lead to a life of addiction. Addiction is a dependence upon an externally derived stimulus to change our body's chemistry in order to change how we feel.

Addiction can never bring lasting peace. Peace comes from the withdrawal of faith in the beliefs that create chemical responses that feel bad. Unless sick, attacked or injured how we feel is caused by what has our faith. What has our faith is our beliefs. A belief cannot enter a believer's mind without a believer's faith. Our beliefs cannot remain within our mind without our faith. Forgiveness is the withdrawal of our faith in beliefs that hold the world and those in it to be responsible for what we feel. *This is why we forgive.* With forgiveness our natural feelings are restored and we no longer require drugs or any other addictive stimulus.

The Sacred Paradox

Each mind has the power to create anything including a 'self'. There are no limits to what we can create. In the moment we define our self, that self establishes the limits of our whole mind's creative expression. Only faith can incarcerate an unlimited mind within an archetypal self that is a Jew, Christian or Muslim. Only faith can create existential and behavioural parameters. Our faith in limitation creates an existential paradox. We must agree to be incarcerated within a limited belief system before we can 'become' an archetypal priest, politician, doctor, chef or soldier.

Each belief prejudices the believer's perception of whatever is defined by their beliefs. Our faith gives our beliefs the power to define and edit what our mind sees. It is not possible to see anything other than our own prejudices when exposed to anything that is defined by our beliefs. Each individual belief has a contextual integrity beyond which that belief has no jurisdiction. When the whole mind is exposed to anything the believer has pre-defined that mind cannot see beyond those prejudices. To believe in something we are told is to *bear false witness*.

Each believer pays the ultimate price when they put their faith in a belief that defines *who* they are. Our faith in a limited self establishes the limits of our mind's expression. The price we pay to be a Muslim,

Jew, Christian, American, Mexican or Russian is the denial of greater understanding. To reject *greater understanding* is to reject the unlimited mind of God. At birth, each child's access to the whole mind is 'unlimited'. The belief in our given identity is a rejection of all but a part of the whole mind. This is a fall from grace. The ego mind is the belief system of an identity.

The mind of the identity is the trespasser referred to in Christian prayer. The *mind of the identity* is referred to by names such as the ego, Satan or the devil. To become the policeman or the criminal we simply acquire a particular set of beliefs. The beliefs act like software that controls the minds expression *from within*. A believer's faith gives any belief permission to enter the mind to 'unconsciously' control the believer. These beliefs are commonly referred to as knowledge. The acquisition of generic beliefs occurs in what we refer to as our childhood or formative years.

What we each believe about our self *we become*. The beliefs are what were once referred to as 'demons'. They were called demons because once they are believed our faith gives them authority to possess our mind. The beliefs are the cause of all suffering in the world. A believer cannot transcend the limitations of their beliefs for as long as those beliefs have the believer's faith. The sacred paradox is that the unlimited believer believed he was a limited *self* that now refuses to withdraw its faith in any belief that the *false self* needs for its continued existence.

How can I escape me and still be me? This is the paradox of a believer who thinks he is an identity. With realisation, the faith that condemned us becomes our saviour. We cannot escape a prison that does not exist. Our spiritual incarceration will continue for as long as we believe what we believe. We must surrender our faith in any belief that defines who and what we are if we are to be *born again*. Our spiritual incarceration can only continue until we withdraw our faith in who we believe we are. Our mind's full expression is restored by withdrawing our faith in all limiting beliefs.

The identity ceases to exist when we withdraw our faith in *who* we define the self to be. Our *false self* must surrender to us its creator and saviour. Our free will was used by others to obtain our mind's faith in a *false self*. To be restored we must transcend all beliefs that have control over our mind's unlimited expression. We are the believer whose faith in our beliefs gave them total control over our whole mind. We are *innocent* because as infants we never chose to believe. When first born our mind was gradually programmed by others with a belief system that replaced us.

Only by withdrawing our faith in our beliefs can we realise *greater understanding*. When we surrender our faith in our false and limited self we are *born again*. The second coming occurs when we *remember* our whole mind. Atonement is the restoration of the separated mind with its father (believer) in heaven (whole mind). Our faith programmed our mind with beliefs that are sins which must be converted. MATTHEW, 18.3, KJV, *"And said, Verily I say unto you, Except ye be converted, and become as little children, ye shall not enter into the kingdom of heaven"*

Thought

We are not thinkers of thoughts. We are the awareness of thought. When we become aware of a thought we may engage with it. Engaging with thoughts may lead to the belief that we are thinking when in fact we are not. Each thought is one of an infinite number of contextually limited possibilities that the mind creates. When our faith installs limiting beliefs within our mind we create a context for the thoughts our mind 'unconsciously' generates. If we engage with a thought it can consume our awareness. When no longer consciously engaged with thought we may say that we had a thought.

When the mind perceives what it defines to be a problem it replaces the experience with what it is perceived to be. To overcome the limitation of the problems that have our faith we created the concept of 'solution'. A belief may be helpful in one context but problematic in another. How our mind perceives the world is determined by our beliefs. The quality of our life is how it feels. How we each define our self and our experience is the cause of what we feel. The 'words' we use to define experience create an instant chemical response that is felt and defined in emotional terms.

Bored, dangerous, scary, difficult, complicated, interesting, exciting, angry, insulted and confused are *not just words*. When we believe that those words are true, our faith alone creates mind-generated 'thoughts' and bodily feelings that manifest a *quid pro quo* in those terms. When believed to be 'true' each of those words is a command to the mind. Our vocabulary creates the mind's perception of experience. Thoughts and feelings are the effect of perception. The words we use to define our self or our experience *immediately* create a chemical effect that is felt.

Most born in freedom can self-programme their own minds within the contexts of *I can* and *I cannot*. An explanation that includes *I cannot* will reveal the limits of comfortable 'voluntary personal expression'. If we contemplate attempting to do what we believe we can or cannot do our mind will *automatically* and *autonomously* generate thoughts to assist or resist our behaviour. These are not 'our thoughts' they are the effect of a cause. The cause of thoughts is the beliefs that sustain perception. The mind cannot create thoughts that exceed a believer's personal vocabulary.

Our response to the question *why* we can't will usually include the word 'because'. Our personal beliefs establish the limits of voluntary individual personal expression. The power of a belief to control what we think and feel is reinforced by *thoughts*. Many children believe in Santa Claus and this creates thoughts that trigger chemical responses that are defined in emotional terms. A child may say that they feel 'excited', 'thrilled' and 'happy'. These feelings are a 'stimulus response' to perception or thoughts and continue until a child withdraws faith in the belief in Santa Claus.

There are macro and micro paradigms and contexts which define the parameters of our collective mind's expression. Complex beliefs require a complex vocabulary. Our mind's faith in the concepts of *'real'* and *'possible'* is the only thing that constrains thoughts to what is believed to be real and possible. Each man is incarcerated by his personal vocabulary. Our personal vocabulary defines our personal reality. When we believe that each word is what it represents, those words replace what is seen with perception. The beliefs are the cause and what the mind perceives is the effect.

Education created a vocabulary that uses faith to install universal beliefs to incarcerate the mind. Our beliefs about our self and experience indirectly create thought. Thoughts are a by-product of our belief system. When our faith defined *this to be this* and *that to be that* our mind perceived those qualities. This and that are 'one' divided by perception. Thoughts and feelings require no conscious effort on our part. If we engage with a thought we may say '*I had a thought*' when in fact we just became aware of a thought. Thoughts and feelings change when our beliefs change.

To be Born Again

I confess to a murder but I cannot be found guilty of the murder I have committed because my victim was me. I killed me when I believed I was what I was told I was. Our creative expression dies with our faith in an identity that places limits within our unlimited mind. The price I paid for a mind that could judge was a mind that could not. When my awareness was free I required no judgement to compassionately express my true self. Before my awareness was incarcerated within the perspective of an identity I required no conscious effort to express language or behaviour.

When our whole mind's awareness is confined to our body's awareness we are gradually convinced that we are the body and its name is *me*. In the moment I believed 'I' was my body my whole mind's awareness was incarcerated by the limits of the body's perspective. My unlimited mind's awareness became limited by the beliefs of a false witness. The body's sight, hearing, touch, smell and taste are limitations that do not exist for me. The mind's interpretation of the body's senses is prejudiced by our faith in 'false witnesses' that are the words of a dictionary.

I didn't realise and was not told that my mind's faith in the identity would give it my authority to control my whole mind. With faith we can move mountains. With the faith of a child's mind we can install beliefs within each child's mind to control the expression of every child. Only the faith of an unlimited mind can incarcerate an unlimited mind. Our faith is our power. Only the removal of our mind's faith can free our mind from the limitations of the beliefs that constrain it. How could we have permitted our unlimited mind to be usurped by the beliefs installed within it?

The question that is used to induce a lifelong trance that incarcerates the awareness of the unlimited mind of the believer is '*What is your name?*' When the child answers with the name of their given identity, the unlimited 'I' that we are in truth becomes limited to *who* I believe I am. *Who* I am is not *what* I am. With our mind's faith we exist vicariously through this limited representative whose perception bears false witness to the experience of the body. What the child does not realise is that the 'I' that they are told is their own identity is not who or what they are.

The identity is an archetypal role that we are expected to play. Policeman, doctor, postman, engineer, terrorist and soldier are typical archetypes. These roles are required by the 'official' paradigms that require those identities for their existence. If we conform to our given identity we are considered normal. If we do not conform to a generic archetype we may be considered odd, heretic, dissentious, slow, criminal, stupid, eccentric, genius or weird. Archetypal roles were created to determine the limits of each mind's freedom of individual expression.

The predominant means of temporary escape from the limited feelings available to an incarcerated mind is 'addiction'. Addictive stimulus provides temporary access to chemical responses that are 'felt' and defined in *emotional* terms that are not available without our body's exposure to that stimulus. Generic behavioural expression

To be Born Again

creates generic chemical responses that we define as our feelings. Through repetition we gradually become oblivious to generic feelings and may look for stimulus or experience that makes us feel higher, happier or better.

Emotional terms define the body's chemical responses to our mind's perception. The quality of our life is determined by 'what we feel'. A good day and a bad day are defined by 'what we feel'. What we feel is caused by how our mind perceives our self and our life. What we feel is determined by how our mind perceives our self and our experience. How we perceive our experience is determined by how our mind's perception defines experience. The only way to transcend the limitations our mind has placed upon our feelings is to 'resurrect' the *believer* that is the 'true self'.

How our mind perceives each experience will determine whether we create 'good' or 'bad' feelings. All 'emotions' are stimulus responses to our mind's perception that are felt. We are deluding ourselves if we call those mind-made pre-determined and pre-rehearsed chemical responses our natural 'feelings'. Emotional responses are mind-made stimulus responses that are felt. Our mind is the creator of each and every psychological condition. We can only torture our self with our mind's hallucinations until we withdraw our mind's faith in those 'perceived' realities.

Our mind's faith in limitation has murdered our innate creative expression. It is because our whole mind's faith is the source of our limited mind that our salvation is assured. To be born again we *must* realise that we are the answer to our prayers. Our whole mind is resurrected when we withdraw our whole mind's faith in each limiting belief. The conversion of each belief leads to our whole mind's salvation. I am forgiven for murder because the commandment stated in EXODUS 20:13, KJV, "t*hou shalt not kill*" is a commandment of God that I *cannot* break.

Each mind is conditioned and domesticated to respond to a name. When believed by me to be me that false witness took my place. I am forgiven because I did not kill me. I did not kill the 'whole' of me because 'I' cannot be killed. If we do not realise the sacrifice we make when we place our mind's faith in our identity, we can be enslaved within this limited perspective for the period of the body's life. The identity is a *sin* and the wages of sin is death. Death is an incarcerated and conditioned mind that controls the whole mind's expression until the child realises and is *born again*.

The archetypes of religion, nationality, politics, vanity and selfishness are 'trespassers'. EXODUS 20:4, KJV, *"Thou shalt not make unto thee any graven image, or any likeness of any thing that is in heaven above, or that is in the earth beneath, or that is in the water under the earth."* EPHESIANS, 5:14, *"Therefore He saith: "Awake, thou that sleepest, and arise from the dead, and Christ shall give thee light."* MATTHEW 18:3, KJV, *"And said, Verily I say unto you, Except ye be converted, and become as little children, ye shall not enter into the kingdom of heaven."*

Tolerance

Overwhelming intolerance is suppressed by our mind's tolerance. Tolerance and intolerance co-exist as separate responses to the same stimulus within the same mind. Intolerance is intolerant of tolerance. Tolerance tolerates intolerance, bullying, force, segregation and racism. Tolerance is passive intolerance that is used to conceal, deny and constrain the overwhelming prejudices that control our collective mind. Tolerance is conditional acceptance. Tolerance qualifies our acceptance. Tolerance is passive intolerance. Passive intolerance creates conflict within the mind. Tolerance is a wolf in sheep's clothing.

Tolerance is not forgiveness. War shows that when our tolerance levels are exceeded our masks fall to reveal intolerance on a global scale. Passive intolerance is not acceptance. What has the mind's faith sustains personal 'tolerance' and 'intolerance'. Authority encourages, nurtures and sustains the killer instinct in man so we will attack and defend. Nothing controls us without our mind's faith. The killer instinct is nurtured with concepts that contextually justify violent acts. Education installs concepts into the minds of children. Concepts are software that remotely controls the mind's responses to qualifying stimulus.

How each mind perceives an experience is determined exclusively by which concepts their mind uses to define that experience. Education is used to gradually nurture and eventually take control of the expression of our collective mind. Religious and moral concepts are used to control the 'mind'. Why control the mind? A conditioned mind controls the resources that are the 'whole mind' and 'body'. Soldiers, terrorists, engineers or doctors are first created within the mind. Religion and education installs concepts within the mind to 'control' man. The church relies upon a child's 'compassion' and 'understanding' to programme their mind.

Religious programming ensures that unless commanded by the church to kill, each 'believer' would only express peaceful words, thoughts and behaviours. When religion decided it was time for the *beast* to kill, it used concepts such as 'blasphemy', 'apostasy', 'heresy', 'unbeliever' and vengeance to justify waking the *beast* in each one of us to kill in the name of God. In each generation there were some who realised 'greater understanding' beyond the jurisdiction of the 'demonic' concepts used by governments and religion. Only a believer's faith can admit a concept into their mind. Our faith allows concepts to control our mind.

Politics is the new disguise worn by the evil forces that corrupt the minds of the parents of the prize. The prize is the omnipotent mind of each child. The concepts of 'equality', 'justice', 'peace', 'patriotism', 'economics' and 'freedom' are used to justify invading lands, displacing, destroying and dispossessing people. So what is tolerance? Tolerance is a temporary state of mind that denies our intolerance until such times as it can be justified. Tolerance is like a muzzle placed on a dog bred for fighting by governments and religion that keeps our hatred alive. Forgiveness is unconditional and permanent but tolerance is conditional and temporary.

The given identity is a 'psychopath' installed by authority within each mind. Faith in our identity grants admission to an archetype. Each conditioned mind is remotely controlled by conceptual programming. Our false (ego) mind is programmed with the concepts of 'charity', 'equality', 'friendship', 'selflessness', 'patriotism' and 'guilt' to ensure that the 'beast' remains dormant within our minds until required to kill and destroy. Concepts such as 'heroism', 'courage' and 'patriotism' or 'cold blooded', 'evil', 'terrorism' and 'racism' describe the same demons using different names. Tolerance is not forgiveness. Forgiveness is our salvation.

We Create Our Life

We can only complain about the quality of our life until we realise that our own mind is creating it. The mind that creates the experience we call our life is *not personal*. The 'whole mind' in which we all exist is a collective resource that is equally available to all. Those of us who wish for a better life haven't realised that our life is the exclusive product of our belief system. Our faith in beliefs about our self and the world replaces both within our mind. Our faith in our beliefs created an operating system that controls the perception and expression of our mind. Education is used to install generic belief systems to control the minds of billions.

The objective of all 'belief systems' is to control and standardise the collective perception and behavioural expression of all. The power of our collective mind is limitless. Our mind delivers what has our faith. What has our faith is our beliefs. When an individual believes *I'm not good enough* the mind will ensure that life's experiences are *never good enough* leading to a life that we may incorrectly say is 'unfulfilled'. What has our faith is whatever we believe. Our faith in our beliefs create a path that we are compelled and fated to follow. Our unlimited mind ensures that our experience does not exceed what has our faith.

Beliefs about struggle ensure we struggle for the

success that our beliefs create. Knowing and understanding that we can do anything is not sufficient to convert our dreams into our direct experience. If we do not have sufficient desire and faith in the belief that we can achieve our dreams they will drift from our awareness and move to the bottom of our mind's 'to do' list. To achieve desires we must *keep them in our awareness*. A burning desire to achieve requires no personal effort or perseverance because there is nothing else we would rather do. We keep the goals that we desire in our awareness without any conscious effort.

Whether by desire, fear or perseverance our mind will create what has our faith. The priority is what has our awareness. Our mind is not personal. Our mind is a miracle that keeps us connected with our source. The judgement we hold about the world is what sustains the world we collectively perceive in our mind. If we judge the world to be boring, difficult, depressing, unfair, cruel and 'messed up' our mind will ensure that we experience the world in those terms. When we give our faith to beliefs that define the world in fixed terms this becomes our world. So our life may feel difficult, depressing, unfair, cruel and 'messed up'.

We are constantly feeling and experiencing the effects of our own judgement in all of our experiences. We are the architect of our own life. Our personal beliefs are like a 'spell' that we cast. What has our faith and our awareness eventually comes to fruition through our life's experience. We must each realise that if our faith is creating the life we are living then our faith has the power to transform our life and our experiences. To know and understand this will not change our experience. We can only realise transformation by withdrawing our faith in beliefs that sustain the existential parameters of the experience that we call our 'life'.

Within our mind we are each simultaneously creating the life we are living. The experience of life is a reflection of what has our mind's faith. Our experience is the effect of our beliefs and our faith is the cause. Why does authority, the media and religion want us to believe their version of truth? The authorities want us to believe their version of 'truth' so that we never realise that each belief proposed by others is a spell that only requires our faith to enter our mind. What converts our dreams or nightmares into our personal experience is 'faith'. The objective of education is to obtain our faith in generic beliefs that will control our mind.

Beliefs sustain existential paradigms. Only our faith allows beliefs to programme and control our mind's expression. Our faith is the most powerful thing in existence. We are the composer of the symphony of our life. We have been tricked into playing someone else's music. We have been tricked into believing that we must learn how to live. We create our world. We are not robots to be trained to dance to somebody else's tune. We realise our power by withdrawing our faith in the dogmatic beliefs that became the 'exclusive author' of the story of our life. We don't have to discover our power because we are the power.

So how is it possible to become a victim of a life that our own mind is creating? We believe we exist in an objective reality that is controlled by authority. Our

What Causes Conflict

faith was used by others to domesticate our mind. Our mind delivers what has our faith. Our life is a reflection of our belief system. Beliefs cannot be placed within our mind by others without our faith. Beliefs cannot remain within our mind without our faith. So if we are limitless how did we come to live in limitation? We placed our faith in limiting beliefs. If we withdraw our faith in limiting beliefs we remove the constraints placed upon our unlimited mind's expression.

What Causes Conflict

Many of our judgements are reflecting archetypal prejudices that exist as our beliefs. How we define everything and everybody is a reflection of the individual beliefs that prejudice our mind. Whether we are angry, frightened, spiteful, kind, friendly, funny, miserable, dangerous, creative or entertaining is determined entirely by the concepts that have our mind's allegiance. Our life is a reflection of the beliefs that have our faith. What has our faith controls our mind. What no longer has our faith is powerless to control our mind. Our mind's understanding creates our experience.

Each concept that has a believer's faith is their mind's witness. Our mind's prior conditioning is superseded with each new belief we acquire *about our self.* Over the period of a lifetime the belief system that controls the mind is revised and updated many times in a similar way that software updates a computer. Beliefs are the cause of all personal and interpersonal conflict. It is only faith placed in beliefs about courage and patriotism that can transform a peaceful mind into a *violent* mind. Man's collective mind is in conflict because we placed our faith in conflicting beliefs.

Terrorism is a testament to the power of faith. Peace is a testament to the power of faith. A phobia is

WHAT CAUSES CONFLICT

a testament to the power of faith. An educated mind is a testament to the power of faith. All conflict is caused by placing our faith in opposing beliefs. Authority, industry and religion create conflicting beliefs each fighting for control of our mind. What has our faith controls our mind. Without faith a belief has no power over a believer's mind. The believer's faith is the believer's power. The first belief *installed* within the mind is the belief in an identity that is installed by others.

As a child, the parent's faith in an identity permits it to enter their mind. This faith compels each parent to install the same archetypal ego identity within their own child's mind. The ego was once called Satan. The *ego identity* can only take up residence within our mind with our faith. All beliefs require a believer's faith to take up residence within a believer's mind. Each generic belief the ego acquires evolves the *false* perspective of an archetypal identity. Each generic archetypal identity consists of a set of generic beliefs collectively referred to as a 'belief system'.

Islam, Judaism, Hinduism, Communism are examples of existential beliefs systems that sustain models of existence. Personal beliefs that are in conflict with archetypal beliefs create dissention, crime and addiction. Each 'personal' belief that is acquired gradually creates a *new* understanding that may be in conflict with the official narrative or understanding. It is because the 'true self' is the believer that by *surrendering to God* we can each save our true self from our false self. It is conflicting beliefs that cause suffering within a believer's mind, body and community.

Until we withdraw our faith in one of any two conflicting beliefs our mind and body will suffer from this conflict. Every belief that has our mind's faith has our power. This is why we are indoctrinated by religion, community, nationality and politics. Beliefs can be creative, evil, destructive, logical, irrational, violent, possessive, greedy, kind, compassionate, helpful and caring. When we place our faith in a belief we self-programme the thoughts and reactions of an *unlimited mind*. A limiting belief will limit us and an empowering belief will empower us.

It is only by withdrawing our faith in one of two or more competing archetypal beliefs existing within us that we can restore peace to our world's collective mind. Our faith can create many conflicting archetypes existing within us. How is it possible to be peaceful in one moment and angry and violent in another? To understand this we must first understand how the mind works. There is one mind with two perspectives, the 'believer' and 'who' he believes he is. Our faith creates an 'archetypal ego identity'. We exist vicariously through an identity that is remotely controlled by beliefs.

Until we realise we are unlimited we will continue to exist vicariously through the limits of the mind of our *given* identity. The beliefs are the limits our faith places on the expression of the mind of our given identity. Our whole *unlimited* mind is controlled by the beliefs we place our faith in. The ego was created to programme the whole mind of each believer so they could be 'remotely controlled' by their beliefs. With our faith the ego that was once called Satan replaces us. In ancient times if the beliefs that had a believer's faith

What is Evil?

were evil they were considered to be *demons*.

Many beliefs are what were once called 'demons' or 'archetypes'. Until we withdraw our faith in beliefs our mind only sees what our mind perceives. To see an enemy we must first believe in the concept of 'enemy'. Our mind can only perceive what we believe. Many beliefs are trespassing within our mind. Some beliefs bear false witness to a reality that is terrifying. Satan is the trespasser. False witnesses are *demonic beliefs* that have our faith. We can only believe what we do not know. Beliefs need our faith because *without our faith they cannot exist within our mind.*

We are not defined by religion, politics or nationality. As our unlimited mind's technological expression demonstrates we are beyond any definition. A good man or a bad man is the effect of the beliefs that have his faith. It is beliefs that are the cause of *all conflict.* In truth, the only good and bad there is, *is the feeling.* If it feels good it is and if it feels bad it is. But what is good for one is not necessarily good for another. Good and bad is therefore subjective. It is subjective because we are each and all unique. *We can do anything!*

If we speak or act without compassion then we may hurt others. Compassion is not the concept of 'pity'. Pity is pity. Compassion is the feelings of others. When we feel compassion it is the feelings of others that is our counsel. Compassion is not psychologically induced emotional responses obtained by looking at a starving child to create self-generated feelings of pity. If our pleasure causes another suffering then we have lost awareness of our innate compassion. With compassion we cannot harm others. Compassion is not a hypothesis to be learned from a special book.

Compassion is the innate ability to feel what others feel. In history, slavery forced many to deny their innate compassion. Over many generations man has been forced to deny his true identity so that his mind could be conditioned to fight in armies and kill others. As demonstrated by a puppy, you domestic the mind by installing a noise that conditions the appropriate behavioural responses. When the believer believes they are their given identity their faith gives that identity control over their mind. The world is in conflict because many beliefs that have our faith are in conflict with each other.

What is Evil?

Evil is a concept. Evil cannot control a believer's whole mind without the believer's faith. The evil that controls the mind *is not in the mind*. It is the demonic concepts that have a believer's faith that cause the believer to do evil. Our mind has been programmed to worship demonic concepts in service of an archetypal identity once called Satan. What is Satan? Satan is the archetypal 'ego' perspective installed within our mind that we mistakenly believe is our identity. A generic archetypal identity is a belief system. Only our faith permits Satan to trespass within our mind.

Satan was created on earth to control the creative expression of man. Our faith in our given identity gives the ego dominion over our mind. God is the divine source of our creative expression. The ego cannot control our mind without our faith. Faith in our *given name* creates an abode for an *identity*. Our faith in 'words' allows education to program our minds. The identity is installed to control the mind's perception and creative expression. With our faith, any concept can be used to control our mind. Satan exists vicariously through a belief system installed by education using words.

The *identity* is a 'spiritual parasite' passed down from generation to generation. Religion and education is used to justify the indoctrination of each child's mind. Children are educated to perceive the world defined by the 'official words' that describe it. Once a word is believed to be what it represents it hypnotises the mind ensuring perception replaces sight. God is misrepresented by words. REVELATION 2:16, KJV *"And he said unto me, It is done. I am Alpha and Omega, the beginning and the end. I will give unto him that is athirst of the fountain of the water of life freely."*

What our mind sees, hears, describes and understands is controlled by our vocabulary. Words are not what they represent. Any word or concept that lacks compassion is not of God but of the ego. The ego uses our faith in concepts to enslave our mind. It is demonic concepts that 'misrepresent' God. If you programme a mind with language then language controls that mind. The dictionary is more powerful than any other book. The words of the dictionary argue for or against the scriptures. The scriptures are questioned *but not the words* used to question or interpret them. *Why is that?*

Without language an incarcerated mind cannot understand. If there is not a word for experience then experience cannot be understood by a mind that is programmed by language. It was our faith in words that permitted language to become the jailor of our mind. When we allow Satan to take our place we are no longer divine. When the slave's behaviour exceeded the control of their masters their children's minds were trespassed against and occupied by a *false ego self* that we each believe is me. With our faith the ego has controlled the collective mind ever since the original sin.

It is because each child's mind is *unlimited* that the world's authorities continue to install the identities that are passed from generation to generation. The mother is the wolf in sheep's clothing, usurped by an *ego* when she was a lamb. As long as each child's mind can be programmed by concepts, concepts will rule the Earth. Any government or religion that uses fear or violence to incarcerate the mind and body is not of God. God is compassion. God is always the *'greater understanding'* that exists beyond all understanding. Any concept that denies compassion is Evil.

What is Forgiveness?

Violent people are living violent lives. Happy people are living happy lives. Simple people are living simple lives and complex people are living complex lives. The quality of our life is how it feels. How our life feels is determined by how our mind perceives reality. Each individual's unique perception is prejudiced by the beliefs that unconsciously operate their mind. For example, two observers could observe the same event and perceive it in different terms. The mind's perception cannot exceed its personal vocabulary. The language of the mind is words and beliefs are its software.

Before the mind can use the voice to describe what the mind perceives it must acquire language. What determines the mind's ability to communicate using language is its vocabulary. Each person's vocabulary and their use of it can vary. How our mind perceives another person is limited by our personal vocabulary. Different people can define the same person to be argumentative, agreeable, intelligent or stupid. Each mind's vision is controlled by its perception. The mind's perception acts like a prescription that creates chemical responses that are 'felt' within the body.

Each emotional response is the body's chemistry responding to the mind's perception. The mind's perception is an instruction to the brain to release

What is Forgivness?

chemicals within the body. For example, a mind that defines 'argumentative' to be bad will create bad feelings when the body encounters argumentative people. The body's chemistry does not respond in emotional terms to an experience but how the mind perceives the experience. If our mind's faith in a concept is withdrawn our body's chemistry cannot respond to any 'stimulus' that conforms to the judgement of that concept.

Forgiveness is the removal of the mind's faith in a belief. The beliefs that affect our body's chemistry are an attack on our peace of mind. The cause of the chemical responses generically defined as feelings and specifically defined as emotions is our mind's judgemental projections. It is the mind's faith in 'moral' concepts that cause the body to respond in those terms. Our body is attacked by chemicals each time we judge *what is* to be less than what it should be. Only the removal of the mind's faith in the concepts that condemn reality can release us from the effects of that judgement.

Christianity was used to justify many concepts used to programme the minds of Christian children. This ensured experience was perceived according to the official concepts used to define people and experience. Many concepts deceive and misrepresent experience. 'Unhappiness' is a 'perceptually induced chemical response'. The *exclusive* cause of the chemical responses that are defined using emotional terms is the mind's perception. When programmed, the mind's perception creates the appropriate stimulus response experienced as thoughts and feelings.

Each emotional response is caused by the personal beliefs that prejudice the mind's perception. All emotional responses are controlled by *how* the mind perceives experience. To control how the mind perceives reality is to control what the mind *thinks* and the *body feels.* We forgive those who trespass against us because their minds are enslaved by their faith in demonic concepts. We forgive our enemies because their minds are enslaved by their faith in beliefs that control what they think and feel. Forgiveness is the withdrawal of our faith in beliefs that lack compassion.

Why Duality?

Duality is created when a believer places his faith in the *belief* that he is what he believes he is. It is in this moment our awareness associates exclusively with one of two perspectives. One perspective is the awareness of our whole consciousness referred to as the 'believer' and the other is the perspective of the body's identity. The thinker and the creator of thoughts are one and the same. Duality is essential if our unlimited mind having no objection or reason is to create thoughts and ideas for the part of our mind in which our awareness is now incarcerated.

We are consciousness. We believe that we are the 'identity' of the body our awareness inhabits. We are not the body. Our faith in our identity incarcerates our awareness within a small part of our own mind. We are both the thinker of the thought and the creator of the thought. Perception, thoughts and ideas are the medium of communication between separate parts of our awareness. The separation that is duality ends when we realise that we are not our body or its 'identity'. We are consciousness. We limit our expression by placing our faith in beliefs about a 'self'.

The beliefs a believer places their faith in create and enforce contextual limits upon the expression of their unlimited mind. Only beliefs can control the expression of a believer's mind. We are the believer! What is the believer? The 'believer' is 'consciousness'. Our faith in the belief that we are our body's identity has incarcerated our awareness within the limits of that perspective. It is the faith we place in our beliefs that controls our mind's freedom of expression. Each parent communicates with their own child's awareness through the eyes and ears of the child's body.

No belief can remain within our mind without our faith. To control the conscious expression of each child's mind you must install a control mechanism. Each child's awareness is conditioned to believe that it is an 'identity'. We are the life of the body. We are consciousness. A 'believer' is created by obtaining our faith in beliefs. Faith ensures each mind *will not* exceed what it believes. Duality is created in the moment that we believe we are the 'identity' that we are told is our whole self. Frustration is caused by placing our faith in beliefs that prevent complete freedom of expression.

The only thing that can limit the expression of a b*eliever's unlimited mind* is *the faith of that believer.* We create duality in the moment we are persuaded to believe that we are the identity of our body. We are not an identity. We are the consciousness that is the life expressed in every living creature. We are born again in the moment that we *realise* our mistake and withdraw our faith in all beliefs that define us. The consciousness of each child is the awareness that sustains all life. Faith in our body's identity caused us to believe that our origin was the location of our body's birth.

Our awareness has not realised that it is conscious-

Why Duality?

ness. A conscious ego mind is created in the moment each body's awareness places its faith in the belief that it is the identity of a body. This is a fall from grace. We become trapped within the perspective of an archetypal identity for as long as we each believe that we are that identity. From the moment we place our faith in our identity we divide our awareness and exist simultaneously within two perspectives. The identity is an illusory perspective sustained only by our faith. Obtaining a child's faith creates a believer.

Unless born disabled or we become ill our limitations are sustained exclusively by the faith we place in our beliefs. Each belief is a limitation. Our beliefs control how and what our mind perceives. Our faith ensures perception limits what we can see and understand. Reality is a concept that defines the parameters of man's collective perception. Consciousness's faith in concepts has incarcerated man within conceptual paradigms held there exclusively by his faith. Separation from our source creates the duality that is essential if our expression is to be controlled by *dogmatic* beliefs.

If a child's mind is unable to accept the 'code of language' required for the *generic archetypal programming* of their mind they will not thrive in a world controlled by language. Language is code. Many who transcend language agree to help others to realise. The risk of conditioning our mind with beliefs is that our acceptance of this programming ensures that our dogmatic faith prevents our own salvation. Realisation is salvation. If we refuse to question who and what we are, we become trapped within limitations that our faith alone creates.

A conditioned mind is an incarcerated mind.

In all jurisdictions each child is replaced by their faith in an archetypal ego identity. Each life is a testament to the power of faith. Our faith is our jailor and our realisation is our salvation. When I believe that I am that, my faith ensures my mind rejects what is not that. We are not the name written on a birth certificate. We are not a religious identity. We are not from any country that is separate to any other country. Our faith in these limitations creates a division within our mind that is reflected in the world. So why do we experience life? The body was created for God to experience life.

It was our faith in limitations that created them. Our faith in hate created it. Our faith in self-created selfishness. Faith in a 'self' separated us from our 'creator'. We are our own creator. We are our own God. Our faith is creating our experiences. Any belief that misrepresents fact is a *sin*. When born, our consciousness is an omnipotent, omnipresent, joyful, compassionate expression of God. An archetypal identity is a rejection of the child God created. Each child is Christ reborn. Faith in an archetypal identity is essential if control of our expression is to be limited by culture and faith.

Our faith in our identity creates the separation referred to as 'duality'. Duality is required if our unlimited mind is to assume the perspective of a 'critical mind'. Why create a critical mind? A critical mind is a mind that uses conceptual criteria to judge *what is* to be less than what it *should* or *could be*. If we do not have a critical mind we will accept what is. If we accept what is, it becomes impossible to continue to evolve in tech-

Why Duality?

nological terms. The survival of animals results from pre-programmed, inherited and acquired instincts that evolve through experience, *not criticism*.

We have already gone through many awakenings in the dream. We realised that we could convert what we created in our mind into our experience. The evolution of our technological expression is demonstrated by archaeologists. If we did not create and evolve a critical mind our technologies would not have evolved in the way they did. When the critical part of our divided mind judged something to be less than what it should be, the other part of our mind responded with thoughts and ideas. Without compassion our ideas may cause suffering. Compassion is *the feelings of others*.

It is a believer's faith in words that exclusively creates perception. Faith ensures that sight is replaced by perception. Each believer's mind is tricked into limited creative expression by placing their faith in 'words' that define concepts. We delegated the power of our mind to the jurisdiction of our beliefs. Duality is essential if we are to consciously harness our creative power. One part of a believer's mind creates thought in response to what another part perceives. Each believer's beliefs define the context and content of the thoughts his mind creates. We *cannot* consciously create thought.

Consciousness is hypnotised by its faith in its beliefs. Only a believer's faith can incarcerate their own creative expression. Each believer's mind must serve the perspective of their identity for as long as they believe that they are that identity. The perspective of the identity creates the illusion that awareness is separated from its own source. Consciousness's *perceived* separation from its own source is impossible. This perceived separation is what some refer to as our 'conscious' and 'unconscious' minds. This division is an illusion existing as a belief made real only by the power of faith.

The identity is a critic installed within our mind to ensure our mind is controlled by our faith in conceptual limitations. A critical mind is necessary if we are to judge and criticise *what is* in technological terms. If we did not divide our mind and use our faith to become our own creation we would have existed as all the other creatures in nature. The technological creativity of other species cannot manipulate the particle or the wave in the same way that man can. The ability to manipulate the earth's resources to manufacture technologies is a symptom of a *sickness* of the mind.

The symptoms of that sickness include selfishness, cruelty, sexual perversions, violence, racism, war, and greed. *Who* we are is the cause of all of the world's suffering. We are not a *who*. Behaviour is not a *who*, it is a *what*. What we each place our faith in is the cause of our individual suffering. For many generations we created an 'archetypal self' in our own image. We continue to create archetypal warriors, gang members, politicians, aristocrats, Christians, Jews and Muslims. The archetypes change as the sickness of our collective ego mind mutates.

The identity is a sickness of our mind created by our own faith. What has our faith has our mind's power. The essence of all religion is our true source. We are that source. Faith in an identity creates a caricature we

Why Duality?

become that exists within our own mind. We cannot fix the world. To transform the world we must heal the mind that creates and sustains our 'perception' of it. We are the truth we seek. Our whole mind is divided in the moment our faith defines our self with beliefs. How our faith defines our self establishes parameters that enforce limits upon our creative expression.

What is beyond the 'self' are the parts of our mind that we deny which creates duality within our own mind. The identity is a part we agree to play. Faith in an identity exiles us within our own mind denying the greater understanding that is our only salvation. In the moment our awareness contemplates greater possibilities our mind generates new *thoughts* and *ideas*. Thoughts lead to realisation. Realisation is our salvation. We can only transcend the limits placed upon our mind by questioning what has our faith. Our mind has no authority to create beyond what we believe is possible.

It is only by obtaining our faith in what is possible that others can place limits upon our unlimited mind's creative expression. There are no limits to the mind's creative potential. Faith gives each belief complete contextual authority over a believer's mind. We are the believer spoken of in scriptures. Our faith gives our beliefs our 'power'. Technological evolution results from the withdrawal of a believer's faith in the historical beliefs that held that form of technological expression to be impossible. The limitations placed upon the mind of historical man were 'dogmatic' beliefs.

Dogma is a limitation that prevents the mind's contemplation or expression beyond the jurisdiction of dogmatic beliefs. These limitations can only exist within the mind for the period of time that they have a believer's faith. We have been told that we are a *who*. If who we believe we are is a warrior then our expression is to kill. The *who* we believe we are is a 'part' our faith creates that controls our own mind. Our faith allows this part to take our place. This part is the 'identity'. For as long as we believe we are our given identity we must exist vicariously through this limited perspective.

The believer is replaced by his own identity in the moment he believes that he is that identity. The placing of our faith in an identity creates a duality within our own mind existing as the believer and the belief. All psychological maladies are caused by the believer giving power over himself to beliefs that create conflict within his own mind. All suffering is caused by placing our faith in beliefs that lack compassion. We are creating our experience. All man made technologies including agriculture, navigation, metallurgy and electronics were first created as ideas in the mind.

For some, when experience stopped short of their personal objective, their faith in the belief that they will do better ensured that their 'unlimited mind' delivered ideas and generated thoughts that showed them how to convert what they believed into what they achieved. Duality is caused within the mind when the believer perceives himself to be what he defines himself to be. Perception is sustained by faith in beliefs. Being whole we are all of our parts. The proposed identity can only take control of our mind when our faith defines this 'archetype' to be our 'whole self' exclusively.

Why Duality?

An identity is an operating system installed within the mind. Our faith gave our identity control over our *unlimited mind*. An unlimited mind has no reason or objection because it is unlimited. For an unlimited mind there is no *good* or *bad*. How we once defined our body's feelings is the origin of the concepts of good and bad. An unlimited mind does not need. An unlimited mind does not want. So what if anything is in control of our unlimited mind? We are! Each belief is a 'spell' cast within our unlimited mind that is held there only by the power of our faith.

Before you can install a belief you need a believer. Until a believer is created the mind is the 'autonomous' expression of a consciousness that has the ability to surpass any technological expression in existence. This means that each one of us has the potential to transform the world. Each new born child is a threat and risk to those who control the world. At some point, some of us decided to control all of us. Anointing a child was the method used by the church to replace the child God created. Rome created an archetype that each man was to be compared with.

To live up to this archetype man had to deny any natural expression that did not conform to his archetypal obligations. The archetype made man insane. The realisation of this is known as being *born again*. In many parts of the world the medium of religion has been replaced by education. Teachers obtain our faith in 'words' that define 'reality'. Education installs knowledge within our mind. Language controls the mind in the same way that computer code controls the creative expression of a computer. The unlimited mind's autonomous expression is what we call life.

So if the mind is unlimited how is it possible to experience sickness and poverty? Unless born ill or injured, all sickness and poverty is first created in the mind. The body is an expression of the mind. The cause of sickness acquired or inherited is the placing of our faith in such limitations. Our faith *exclusively* controls the expression of our own mind. Before our faith was used to programme our own mind we reacted to how our experience felt. Language creates 'feelings' by harnessing the creative expression of our mind. The life that is expressed in each body is *consciousness*.

In history, slavery and violence were used as methods to harness and control behavioural expression. Slave rebellions demonstrate that a free mind cannot be tamed. Religions used a child's faith to take ownership of their mind's 'perception'. The objective of the church was to control the expression of the *unlimited mind* expressed in each and every child. Religions knew that to replace a child within its own mind you must obtain their faith in an archetypal identity. Those who are looking to politicians and the church for guidance have not realised.

The method used to *usurp* each child within its own mind is to obtain their faith in the belief that they are an identity. *Only what we do not believe* will save us. Faith is the most powerful thing in existence. MATTHEW 17:20 KJV *"And Jesus said unto them, because of your unbelief: for verily I say unto you, If ye have faith as a grain of mustard seed, ye shall say unto this mountain, Remove hence to yonder place; and it shall remove; and nothing shall be impossible unto you."* In history when a child was born it was told that

Why Duality?

it was the function it was required to fulfil.

Our faith in our identity denies us the purity and freedom of our own life. In history, the function of blacksmiths, carpenters and wheelwrights was their name. Duality refers to two perspectives. One perspective is the 'unconscious' whole mind. The other perspective is the consciously expressed part of that mind that is programmed by beliefs. We have delegated our whole mind's authority to the jurisdiction of our beliefs. Our whole mind creates in response to our 'perception'. Our perception is the cause of our thoughts and our beliefs are the cause of our perception.

Until we realise, we will continue to exist vicariously through the perspective of a role our faith created and now sustains. Our faith created an existential paradox. The role we play is the identity. This identity is a part we are given to play in an adventure that we call our life. We play this part completely. We are not the role we play. We are the creator of our identity. The identity is fiction, not fact. Our faith in this perspective created it. The identity's memory commences in the moment it comes into existence. The mind of our identity does not know that it is its creator's jailor.

The mind of the identity can only remember what occurred from the moment it was created. We created the ego in our own image. It has no memory of its creator. We are incapable of fear. What fears is the ego. What does the ego fear? The ego fears that God will realise and take his rightful place. This is insane because we are the God our ego mind fears. This is why we must surrender to God. One of the perspectives our awareness assumes is that of the body. It is only by placing our faith in limitations that our unlimited mind can exist in limitation. Faith in God is our only 'salvation'.

We are the consciousness of the body. This makes us the true perspective and the life of the body we inhabit. We believe we are our given identity. *We can only believe what we do not know.* We are the creators of the experience that we call life. The beginning of our life within the body is birth and the end of our mortal incarceration is death. This is what we call life. As our awareness of the collective perspective evolved so did our ability to relate with other bodies sharing the experience of life. When we developed language we were able to define what we were experiencing.

When language was used to define people we replaced what we were with what we perceived ourselves to be. Our technological evolution is proof of the power of our mind. War, hunger and poverty are proof of the power of dogma. When children were persuaded to believe that they were what they were told they were, their faith alone created constraints upon the expression of their 'unlimited mind'. Faith in 'dogma' ensures that each believer relinquishes control over the expression of their own mind. We are the life that medical instruments detect. When we are gone the life is gone.

So what is thought? Thought is a symptom of a conditioned mind. A thought offers an alternative possibility. A thought created by one part of the mind can frighten the other part that becomes aware of it. A thought can inhibit or liberate us within or beyond perceptual constraints enforced by our faith. Conscious-

Why Duality?

ness has no reason or objection and does not think, judge or reject. So, how do we think, judge and reject? Consciousness believed it was someone who can. When consciousness believed it was a person who thinks, judges and rejects, it created a surrogate. *The ego!*

We are the 'one consciousness' expressed in all life. We are sociable because it is our own self that we communicate with when encountering what we perceive to be other individuals. Each body is a unique expression of one consciousness. So you are me and I am you. We are! We do not need noise to express our self or to understand the expression of others. There is only one mind communicating with itself. The identity is a part of the whole perceiving itself as separate by individually identifying with separate parts of itself. One can be divided by an infinite number of parts.

We are the God that created the ego in our image. Our faith gave this false self our power and when we believed we were it, *it took our place.* We gave it free will. Our life is a testament to the beliefs that have *the ego's* faith. Each body is contextually separate from other bodies. If we remove the context we remove the separation. This separation is created by faith and sustained by perception. When I perceive my leg to be separate from my arms I lose awareness of the whole. This is how the mind created duality. Each mind is consciousness. There is only one consciousness.

When consciousness looks through the eyes of one perspective it can see the body of another perspective. Faith in beliefs was used to perceive those other perspectives to be different and separate. Contextually the separation of the bodies is fact. Contextually the separation of cells in the body is fact. Our perception of self was the creation of the perceiver and the perceived, the creator and creation. There is only the unlimited self. This is the truth of each one of us. In truth we have no desire. The truth of us is that we need and want nothing and that we are incapable of feeling fear.

I am is our personal truth. Anything that follows 'I am' is an attempt to define and therefore limit 'what' I am. We are the one consciousness expressed in all new born children. Soon after the birth of the body we begin to hear noises. We each hear a noise that we are told is our true identity. This noise has no meaning until we believe that we are the noise that is the given name. Before I could be conditioned to respond to my given name or confirm that I am my given identity, I had to believe that it was me. This was the creation of an archetypal me *within my own mind.*

The creation of a second version of each one of us is essential if we are to judge *what is* to be less than what it should be. The ego created a paradox. How can an unlimited mind experience limitation? *It cannot!* When an unlimited mind believes that it is limited it creates paradox. Consciousness is an expression of an unlimited mind. Only the child's own faith can replace itself with an identity. Each child is 'educated' to ensure that it is constrained by its own faith. Technological evolution is possible by placing our faith in beliefs that judge *what is* to be less than what 'it' should be.

The limited part of our divided mind criticises what it perceives and asks questions. It is the whole unlimited mind that responds to our perception with thoughts and ideas that *cannot* exceed what we believe is possible. So this other part of our mind responds to our questions. In some therapeutic contexts this is referred to as the 'conscious mind' and the 'unconscious mind'. In some contexts this is referred to as the 'mind' and the 'higher mind'. This is also referred to as 'duality'. The impossible became possible when we removed the limits our faith placed upon what is possible.

Zero

When we realise our potential we inherit a gift that cannot be lost or stolen. Whilst potential has no objective value *its intrinsic value is priceless.* When our life is compared with our 'heart's desire' it reveals if we are fulfilling or squandering our potential. What we create is an expression of our potential *but it cannot define it.* The potential of each one of us is beyond any value or object that can be defined or quantified. Zero is unlimited. Zero is infinite. This means that zero is always more valuable than any object or quantity that it is compared against. Zero is the value of the entire universe. Zero is the value of all potential.

No amount of gold can equal the value of the mind's potential. Alchemy is our faith's conversion of our dreams or our beliefs into our life experience. Potential is unlimited because zero is unlimited. If our potential is unlimited then how can the expression of some appear limited? *Each life is always the 'direct effect' of faith.* Each person's unique expression reflects what has their faith. Placing our faith in limiting beliefs gives those beliefs complete control over the expression of our mind and body. Because the world only values what can be 'perceived' faith has no value in the world. Nothing is more powerful than faith.

Zero is a metaphorical drawing board in our mind

that is an unlimited resource. The value of the mind is its potential. An empty mind is unlimited because an empty mind is *free*. It is the quality of an experience that is its 'value'. The quality of an experience is how it feels. In all situations our body's sensory memory unconsciously records the 'perceived cause' of our body's feelings and uses those 'feelings' to programme *sensory perception*. Each body's sensory memory sustains *sensory perception*. Perception triggers sensory memory to recreate the same feelings that were felt in an original experience when we re-experience it.

Sensory memory can cause the body's feelings to respond to perceived harmful stimulus with fear. Our perception creates prescriptions for neurochemicals that our brain instantly dispenses. Neurochemical changes are 'feelings' and emotions'. Perception acts like a security camera that triggers a switch that immediately changes the brain's chemistry. Phobic perception triggers chemicals that prevent our body's freedom of expression. In neurological terms these are neurochemical changes. The chemical changes we feel allow us to avoid perceived danger by guiding us towards or away from *pre-defined* stimuli.

The origin of 'good' and 'bad' was how an experience felt. It is by using language to define the cause of our feelings that we *consciously* programme our perception. Once we define an experience to be 'good' or 'bad' our perception creates matching neurochemical responses to future qualifying stimulus. *Educated perception* can cause *psychological complexes*. In psychological terms we define neurochemical changes to be 'perceptually induced emotional responses'. For centuries, psychological complexes were created and sustained by the Church whose dogma replaced natural sensory perception with *religious perception*.

In fact the only 'good' and 'bad' there is, is the feeling! Before our natural expression was controlled by 'psychologically induced emotional responses' our natural feelings were our guide. We are living proof that this natural guidance kept our ancestors alive. Our feelings reveal to us if we are hot or if we are cold. Our body's natural responses are great teachers. Our natural guidance is our feelings. Health is a feeling. Illness is a feeling. Love is a feeling. Pain is a feeling. All feelings are *teachers*. Pain is the most powerful teacher of all. The natural guidance of our feelings is what some refer to as our 'natural instincts'.

If we feel bad around something we naturally avoid it. When we feel a strong desire towards something we are attracted to it. These natural instincts existed before we developed language. Language has enabled us to evolve a vocabulary that is vast enough to define everything seen in existence. The creation of the word 'bad' enabled us to create 'bad feelings' in others simply by obtaining their faith in our words. CORINTHIANS 5.7 KJV *"For we walk by faith, not by sight"*. One person's faith may perceive an experience to be enjoyable whilst another person's faith may cause them to perceive the same experience to be terrifying.

Words can describe something or someone as 'good' or 'bad'. If our testimony is believed by others it will define their perception which will programme their brain's chemical responses. It is our own perception that denies us our own happiness. We must all realise how our testimony can influence the perception and feelings of others. EXODUS 23:1 KJV "*Thou shalt not raise a false report: put not thine hand with the wicked to be an unrighteous witness.*" The ability of our feelings to respond to the words of others has been used by many to create 'psychologically induced emotional responses' resulting in complexes, fears and phobias.

A phobia creates a personal prison within the mind that is powerful enough to constrain the strongest of men. A phobia is the effect of a belief. A belief requires a believer. Each believer has complete control, power and dominion over their own unlimited and omnipotent mind. Our mind has complete control over our own body. Paradoxically our faith in the belief that we are powerless uses our own feelings to suppress our power. It was Samson's belief that he was powerless without hair that caused his powerlessness. God creates what has our faith. Samson's faith was his strength. It was Samson's beliefs that were his weakness.

Faith can move mountains. Only faith can sustain a psychologically induced fear or phobia. Faith is what turns an aspirant into a master. *I can't* is a powerful spell that is 'blasphemy'. *I can't* are the words of a belief that usurps a believer with his own power. A believer's power is his faith. Powerlessness is a delusion that ends when we withdraw our faith in all beliefs that limit us. What follows *I am* reveals the beliefs about our self that have our faith. Our words can affect our self and others. We can inspire or we can intimidate. We intimidate others by obtaining their faith in testimonies that manipulate their brain's neurochemistry.

Doubt is a feeling that is a dilemma caused when thoughts, beliefs and feelings are in conflict. A doubt may be felt by an individual when there is an obligation or desire to engage in an activity that they have been educated to believe or know to be 'wrong'. The zero of our potential is replaced by our life's expression which is the fruit that reveals what has our faith. Any belief that uses our brain's neurochemical function to prevent our freedom of expression is *unworthy of our faith.* What trespasses within our mind are archetypal beliefs that programme fearful neurochemical responses preventing our complete freedom of expression.

All beliefs are plagiarising experience. *We can only believe what we do not know!* When we lose people to disease, war and violence we can form certain beliefs about those situations. Experience means that we 'know'. Only experience can prove or disprove an academic hypothesis. Academic knowledge is beliefs that have faith. We only truly know what we experience. Educational knowledge requires our faith in what is taught or written. Educational *knowledge is not what is known, but what is believed.* A believer is incarcerated within their own mind by placing their faith in beliefs that limit their own creative expression.

The period of a believer's existential incarceration is equal to the period of time that their limiting beliefs have their faith. Children are educated to place their faith in beliefs. Systemic beliefs are taught in schools to generically programme the *perception of entire countries.* Religion and society expects parents to enforce behavioural compliance in infants with limited cognition by teaching them manners. Generic education obtains a child's faith in archetypal beliefs created to protect, control and manipulate them. An example of a belief created for protection that requires a child's faith is that they 'should not talk to strangers'.

Examples of beliefs placed within our mind to control and manipulate us are those promoted by propaganda, religion, politics and the class and caste system. The beliefs placed within a child's mind can only control what they think and what they feel if the child's faith believes them to be fact. Faith can move mountains. *What is faith?* Faith is our God given *power*. What we believe has our faith. What has our faith has our power. If I believe *I cannot* or *should not* then my faith in those limitations is unrivalled in its power to constrain my mind and body. A believer is the source and power of all faith! *We are all believers!*

There is no one person that has more faith than any other. The faith of each one of us is *equal*. Each and every one of our beliefs has our personal faith. Our faith gives our beliefs full control over our mind and body in the world. A belief has no power without faith. No limitation can remain within our mind without our faith. If I hate you, then hate has my faith. *'Forgiveness is the removal of faith in beliefs'*. Our salvation or damnation is caused by what has our faith. Faith cannot exist without a believer. Salvation is the *reward* that comes from withdrawing our faith in all beliefs that incarcerate us within our own mind.

Faith is the most powerful thing in existence

because without faith a proposed belief has no power over a believer. A murderer, preacher, teacher, politician, loving parent or rapist are unique expressions that have *equal faith*. It is only by placing our faith in beliefs that lack compassion that we become capable of committing acts that are selfish, cruel, perverse and evil. All suffering is caused by placing our faith in beliefs that lack compassion. Any religion or government that deliberately obtains the faith of children in archetypal beliefs created to prevent their unique creative expression are lacking in both wisdom and compassion.

We are not a religious identity. We must stop programming our children's minds with educational beliefs or religious dogma created to remotely control their creative and behavioural expression. If one of us has an experience that feels 'good' we may tell others. We may use 'conceptual terms' to describe an experience and how it felt. An honest description of an experience as boring, exciting, terrifying, great, disgusting, joyous, easy, difficult, appropriate or inappropriate may be truthful but not factual. Over time we have increased the vocabulary that we use to universally define our experiences.

If we place our faith in the testimony of someone who from a single experience defines in absolute terms that type of experience then we deny our self the truth of our own experience. The truth is how we feel. When we define an experience by what we feel we may be truthful but not factual. An individual's subjective experience cannot objectively define that experience. The truth of an experience is how it feels. The truth is *not fact*. The truth is to speak with integrity according to our understanding. A wise man and a fool can both speak truthfully. An honest and truthful testimony may or may not include objective facts.

When my 'perception' of an experience is based upon the testimony of someone else I deprive myself of *my truth*. The personal truth of an experience is how it feels. When someone else tells us an experience is 'enjoyable' we will only take their testimony as fact, *if we believe them. We can only believe what we do not know.* The brain does not differentiate between the mind's 'educated perception' (belief) or the body's 'sensory perception' (fact). For example, the brain can perceive fiction as fact creating neurochemical changes. A 'sad' or 'scary' movie manipulates the brain to create 'perceptually induced emotional responses'.

A phobia is caused by what we believe about an experience. A belief about an experience can create joyful or phobic responses without ever having the experience. How we define an experience is either based upon 'what we believe about an experience' or the experience. There is no substitute for the experience because the experience is *the experience*. Zero is the potential of a mind that has no beliefs. Beliefs are no substitute for truth. Personal truth is no substitute for objective facts. The experience is the *truth* of the experience. The truth of an experience is how it feels. How it feels for one may differ to how it feels for another.

A belief about an experience that we have never experienced can determine how we think and feel about that experience. When we have a belief about an experience our feelings will respond to our 'perception' of the experience but not the experience itself. For example, if we have a belief that an activity is 'dangerous' and then attempt to engage in that activity our feelings respond to how that belief has programmed our perception. Cognitive perception is not vision it is the projection of personal prejudices sustained by personal beliefs. Perception is a veil that acts like a filter that prevents our awareness of *greater understanding.*

We can only believe what we do not know. A mind that is full of beliefs about things for which a believer has no experience is prejudiced. Limiting or fearful beliefs inhibit potential. An empty mind is full of possibilities. Zero is our potential. Our beliefs are constraints that our faith places upon the expression of our unlimited potential. When zero is replaced by our faith in a Muslim, Jewish or Christian identity, our faith ensures that the expression of our potential is *prescribed.* No value is greater than zero. It is because manifested reality is the only thing that can be detected or measured that zero is considered to be less than one.

An ascetic is not someone who abstains. An ascetic is someone who is 'fulfilled'. An ascetic has everything they need. If we have everything we need then we need nothing. When we need nothing and we have nothing *we are fulfilled*. All values are the potential of zero. Without zero there could be no potential. Being its source, zero cannot add to one. One is our identity claiming to be what zero became. *We are all individual expressions of zero!* Only our 'personal faith' can place limits upon our mind's creative expression. Zero is the source of all values. Zero is the canvas of our mind that illustrates everything in existence.

When our faith converts our dreams into our life experience the canvas of our mind still exists as an unlimited source and resource. When the poor man becomes rich his potential is unaffected. When the rich man loses it all his potential is unaffected. Zero and one exist simultaneously. Those who value one more than zero have not realised that zero is infinite. Anything that can be consumed can be destroyed. Only a possession can be lost or stolen. It is because we lost awareness of the miracle that is the source of our 'unlimited potential' that we only value what can be lost, stolen or destroyed. *We are the miracle!*

Ten, a hundred, a thousand or a million cannot exist without zero. When all riches are gone Zero remains. Zero cannot be taken, stolen or destroyed. Zero is indestructible. Zero is all potential value. Our fate is only affected by what has our faith. Technology demonstrates how our faith has manipulated the particle and the wave. The perceived world and the body that experiences it are ephemeral but *zero is not*. Zero is the unconscious potential of all life. In essence we are each a zero with the potential to evolve into anything. The only limits that can be placed upon our personal expression are those that our faith alone creates.

If we lost everything that we own and everyone that we love, there is still *potential*. It is only by comparing zero with something that exists in the world that its value can be diminished. Our achievements in life establish the limits that we alone have placed upon our personal expression. Those who have little or no material wealth may have still realised their potential. Fulfilment is realised potential. What is fulfilment? Fulfilment is the attainment of peace of mind and body. Those with the least amount of wealth and possessions have the greatest potential. MATTHEW 5:5 KJV, "*Blessed are the meek: for they shall inherit the earth.*"

We cannot lose zero but we can lose our awareness of it. Those who value one more than zero have not realised that the potential of zero is unlimited. Zero is always more valuable than anything 'seen' in existence. What can be stolen or lost is not as precious as zero because zero cannot be lost or stolen. LUKE 12.33-34 KJV "*Sell that ye have, and give alms; provide yourselves bags which wax not old, a treasure in the heavens that faileth not, where no thief approacheth, neither moth corrupteth For where your treasure is, there will your heart be also.*" Only our beliefs empowered by our faith can reject our divine inheritance.

Zero is the unlimited non-existing *pre-existence* of all potential. It was because our divine inheritance which is the power of our faith could not be taken from us that we were educated to place our faith in limiting beliefs. Faith in limitation is why some exist without food or shelter. Each person's experience reveals what has their faith. Few have realised that our faith *always* converts our unlimited potential into our life experi*ence. In life, what we believe* about our self we become! Salvation of the *whole self* is the highest achievement of man. Salvation cannot be bought, found, learned, lost or stolen. It can only be *realised*.

End

You can find more information
and essays at my website

www.themessagewoaaa.com

www.ingramcontent.com/pod-product-compliance
Lightning Source LLC
Chambersburg PA
CBHW022110040426
42450CB00006B/650